Sinclair Tousey

A Business Man's Views of Public Matters

Sinclair Tousey

A Business Man's Views of Public Matters

ISBN/EAN: 9783337216085

Printed in Europe, USA, Canada, Australia, Japan

Cover: Foto ©Suzi / pixelio.de

More available books at **www.hansebooks.com**

A

BUSINESS MAN'S VIEWS

OF

PUBLIC MATTERS.

BY

SINCLAIR TOUSEY.

NEW YORK:
THE AMERICAN NEWS COMPANY,
121 NASSAU STREET.
1865.

PREFACE.

—o—

The theory of our Government is that each man is a part of it, or rather that each is supposed or expected to take part in its affairs. This not only confers privileges but demands duties. I have occasionally, through the newspapers of the day, contributed a mite towards the promotion of what appeared to me to be such a state of public opinion as would conduce to the greatest good of all our people. Perhaps I may be charged with egotism in reproducing these views in this form, but desiring to preserve them, and presuming that a few of my friends might read them, I have caused their publication in this shape. I submit them as the views of one of the people on the topics discussed, and if they have been or may be of any use, I shall be satisfied.

SINCLAIR TOUSEY.

New York, July, 1865.

ON STRIKES.

[The following remarks on the subject of Labor Strikes were made in 1859, before a Debating Society, and were printed in pamphlet form by request of the Society.]

I am opposed to Labor Strikes. I believe their results are injurious to the strikers and useless to the community. I grant the abstract right of workmen to demand increased pay for their work, but deny their right to force any person into combinations for that purpose. Such force is injurious to the forced ones, by depriving them of a chance to work for their living, and compelling them either to subsist on charity or consume in idleness the savings of former labor. Combined strikes and trades' unions do this, when they require their members to stop work, because increased wages are demanded. This was the case at Lynn, where the "Scabs" (those who would work for what they could get being thus called) were daily visited by the strikers' committee, and coaxed and threatened to desist from work. This is wrong. Strikes can never permanently benefit the strikers. Why? Because they are not based on correct principles. The price of labor, like that of all other saleable articles, must be regulated by supply and demand. This is proved by the fact that the same labor commands more pay in one place than in another. California furnishes proofs of this. When the first rush took place to that State, in 1847, day laborers commanded five times as much for their services as they now get. Why? Simply because that in 1847 the demand was in excess of the supply, and as the supply increased, as it is always sure to do under high wages, the wages were correspondingly reduced.

This must ever be so ; were it different, two very great injuries would result : First, the maintenance of *high prices* must, of necessity, be *at the cost of the consumer* of labor products ; and secondly, if competition be not allowed in the labor market (as it could not be if supply and demand did not regulate prices) injustice, must be done to those who would compete for the labor ; and this injustice deprives these parties of the work they would be glad to do. So we must come back to letting supply and demand regulate prices, and this law can never be set aside by strikes.

Take another view of the principle involved in this system of strikes. A store in Wall street rents for ten times as much as a similar one in Eighty sixth street. Why ? Simply because the demand for stores in Wall street is ten times as great as is the demand for stores in Eighty-sixth street. Now suppose the landlords of Eighty-sixth street were to apply the principle of strikes, and demand the same rent as the landlord of Wall street, does any man suppose they would succeed ? We all know they would not, simply because the law of demand and supply is superior to the landlords; so it is in the case with labor, and, therefore, labor strikes can never override these laws. They are as immutable as the principles of cause and effect.

Take another view. The consumers of any given article far outnumber the producers of that article. In some cases, perhaps, there are fifty consumers to one producer. Now, any strike or other cause that enhances the price of this product is at the cost of the consumer, for we all know that it is the consumer who eventually pays for all labor and profit of production ; and the hatter who has to pay more for his shoes in consequence of an advance caused by a strike, must in his turn ask higher prices for his hats ; and so with the tailor and others ; and if these cannot get advanced prices for their labor, all advance made to the shoemaker for his labor must be at the cost of these other workers ; and this certainly is unjust to them, for its effect is to depreciate their labor by requiring more of it to buy their shoes.

So it is with all branches of industry and every class of consumers ; all advances in the cost of manufacturing an article are at the expense of the consumer, and as there must always be more consumers of manufactured articles than producers, their interest must not be overlooked in any proposed change. Strikes never benefit the consumer. The producer of one product is of necessity the consumer of some other product, hence the interest of the consumer is greater. Again : the system of strikes is unjust to the best workmen, even under the "piece" system, by compelling a uniformity of prices for anything that will pass inspection. This dulls the spur of ambition to excel in the quality of work, destroys the principle of "reward to merit," and places the passable botch on a par with the most perfect workman, all of which is at the cost of the consumer ; therefore I oppose these strikes. I believe in letting good work bring more than poor. Strikes place all on a common level, *provided* the work merely bears inspection.

It is said that the prices paid for work are not sufficient for the support of the workers. This proves that too many are engaged in that kind of work. The proper and only way to remedy that is, for some of those workers to quit that branch and follow others. But I am told that all branches are over-crowded with workers. But I deny that all branches are thus overstocked with labor everywhere. This overstock is confined to localities, and is not universal. This is proved by the fact that the same labor commands much higher prices in one place than in another, simply because demand and supply are different in these localities ; and strikes will never equalize or regulate these differences of localities.

Again. There are no laws compelling men to continue in work that pays so poorly, and if they continue in it, it shows that they can (being ruled by interest) do better at that than anything else, or they would not follow it. Therefore, strikes are useless.

Again. If the surplus of labor by competition for work has reduced wages to a low figure, which in its turn has increased the stock of manufactured articles on hand, how can you expect an increase of wages to all those workers, in the absence of an increased demand for their products? It is impossible; if you lessen the number of workers, and the demand for their labor is not decreased, it would be reasonable to demand increased pay ; in fact, such decrease of the laborers would command an increase of their pay (though at the cost of the consumer) ; on the other hand, if the number of workers remained the same, and there should be an increased demand for their products, then their pay might be increased ; thus again proving the omnipotence of supply and demand in regulating prices.

Strikes never add to consumption of manufactures, and of course cannot permanently add to wages ; strikes decrease consumption, and thus injure the business of others.

While the shoemakers of Lynn are on a strike they cannot consume the coats, hats, &c., of the other mechanics of their town, and these others being curtailed in the sale of their labor in manufactured articles, cannot buy of the producers of provisions and luxuries as much as formerly, and we of New York, who act as the go-between of both consumers and producers, are curtailed in our business. Therefore, I oppose these strikes as injurious to all classes of community and beneficial to none.

I have said that if wages were advanced by strikes, it must be at the cost of the consumer. I will illustrate this in a home case. In this city there is a baker and miller, who, by the aid of capital and machinery produces flour and bread cheaper and better than any other man in the city. Now, I believe that good flour and cheap bread are of the utmost importance to the consumer, (and these articles are consumed by the entire public), especially the poor. The other millers and bakers attempted to apply the principle of strikes to this man by entering into a compact to see if they could not get him to sell as dearly as they did. He was not influenced by them, and went on selling bread and flour cheaper than the others. Now, suppose these strikers had gained their points, at whose cost would it have been? Why, the consumer must have paid the extra price.

So with all strikes when successful in their demands; hence I am opposed to them. If they fail in getting the advances demanded, they entail enormous expenses of money and loss of time on the strikers, and therefore I oppose them.

I am told that the tailors may strike for higher wages—I hope not. It is said, in excuse for the contemplated strike, that their wages are too low. Will strikes lessen the ultimate number of tailors or increase the ultimate demand for their work? If neither, then a strike will be injurious to them. There are many causes for the low price of needlework, by which I mean all work done by the needle, and the most controlling in its effects on prices for ordinary work on vests, pants, and cheap coats, is the immense amount of work done by the wives and daughters of thousands of farmers and others living near our big cities. Wagon-loads by the score of this work are done weekly by these people, and must continue to be thus done. Strikes will not lessen their number one single person; in fact, a strike among the tailors would have the effect to increase their number, and as these persons live cheaper than can our city tailors, the chances are that, once embarked in the work, it would be very difficult for the tailors to get the work out of their hands again; in fact, it would be almost impossible, for now, while the tailors are at work, these country workers are powerful competitors, and they would be much more powerful by an increase of their number, and they would surely thus increase, should the city workers stop and carry on a strike. But, say our city tailors, we can drive these people out in the future, if we don't succeed in our strike, by resuming work again at the old rates. Not so, my friends. These country workers, having left their callings to make cheap clothing, will, in self-defense, stick to it, for their former work is now done by others. Don't you see, my friends, that this striking is not all on one side. It is a two-edged sword. It cuts two ways.

I told you that if strikers succeed in getting advanced wages it must be at the cost of the consumer. Friday papers furnish me proofs of this:

CABINET MAKERS' UNION.—On Wednesday evening a meeting of cabinet makers and manufacturers was held at Central Hall, Mr. Schoenenberger in the Chair. The organization of a Bosses' Union was completed, with a view to protecting the interests of the trade in the maintenance of a uniform standard of prices, to enable them to pay the wages demanded by the journeymen.

This is to the point, and this must always be the result. Strikes benefit no one. A few words as to the cost of strikes. The Lynn shoemakers have expended in cash, saved from former earnings, some $10,000, a part of which was used for music, banners, dances, processions, etc. The time lost in idleness would have brought them, even at the low wages they complained of, at least $30,000 more, making $40,000. Now, how long will it take them, supposing they get the advanced prices they demanded, to earn this immense sum *over and above* what they were getting before they struck, and how long will it take them to make up this great loss at the old wages? Don't you see that strikes are extremely costly as well as wholly useless?

Trades' unions and strikers' combinations have advocated the requiring of three years' apprenticeship before men can have work at established prices. This at first sight looks well, as inducing good workmen; but there are other views of this matter. Some men are better qualified by taste, genius, and inclination, to perfect a job after one year's instruction, than others are at three, and to compel the former to work as apprentices as long as the latter is highly unjust. When a man can do work well he ought to have the best prices, whether he has worked one month or ten years under instruction. That is the only true and just principle of apprenticeship.

Again. To prevent persons from working at any trade who have not served a given time as pupils is to prevent competition and deprive these of opportunities to earn their living, and this at the cost of persons who consume the products of such labor. Many mechanics leave families unprovided for at their death. Among them are half-grown lads, who, by a little training (not three years) and the spur of necessity, may soon produce as good a hat, or boot, or coat, or lay as many bricks, as did their father, the dead mechanic. Now I assert that these boys are entitled to all they earn, just as much as is the man, whether they have served longer or shorter as apprentices, the only test being the production of equal amounts of equally good work.

Strikers' and trades' unions prevent such a fair system of pay for so much labor, by demanding long apprenticeships. They are all unjust. They have grown out of that old and nearly exploded idea of the people looking to some person beyond themselves to take care of them. Trades' unions and strikers' combinations are the off-shoots of the idea that people must look to governments or societies to see to them. Their tendency is to destroy the principle of self-dependence, reliance on one's own self, on one's own capacity to stem the tide of life's struggles, to destroy all individuality, to deaden all personal ambition, and to blot out all those great efforts by which a man works his way up and over the difficulties that meet him in the battle of life. These societies sink the man in the mass, deprive him of ambition to excel, beget in him a feeling of dependence on something besides himself, foster in him that slavish idea of "*I can't do anything*," instead of encouraging that other and nobler idea, "*I will do everything.*" All such societies and combinations are bad, bad, bad. Mr. Draper, of Lynn, stated at the Cooper Institute, in asking for money to aid the strikers, that there were in his town 300 indigent shoemakers out of work, supported by charity.

Now just see what injustice the strike did in this case. These 300 men wanted work; they needed work; they could not live without work; yet these strikes compelled those poor men to stop earning their bread; and not satisfied with this they actually compelled them to subsist on charity; and still worse, if possible, they really taxed those who had something to live on, with the support of these 300 indigent men; and after using up all they could beg at home for their support, these strikers actually sent beggars all over the country to beg of hard-working men money to support these 300 paupers in idleness; and this man, Draper, pretending to be a *free* American workingman, had the audacity to stand before a New York audience of laboring men and ask for money to support these idlers, not from choice, as he tells us, but idlers by the demands of these strikers; and that, too, in face of the fact that the cessation of these men from work must have the positive effect to increase the price of the articles made by the strikers, and consumed by those whose money they were begging. Thus it is with strikes. The workers of this city ought to have sent Draper home with his pockets as empty as his head.

We are told that the bosses are always ready and willing to oppress the workmen by low wages, and sympathy is demanded for the men. This is a false issue; there is no sense in it. It involves the idea of classes, and fosters unwise prejudices, and separates communities by making fictitious distinctions. The boss of to-day is in this country the journeyman of to-morrow, and the journeyman of to-day is the employer of to-morrow. We have no castes or classes, with exclusive privileges, not open to all alike. The interest of the worker cannot be separated from that of the employer; one is dependent on the other, and neither can exist alone. Hence, all ideas calculated to prejudice one against the other injure both.

Again. The journeymen are just as apt to attempt to oppress the bosses by asking more pay, as are the bosses, on the other side, to attempt to oppress the journeymen by reducing their wages. They both act from self-interest, each trying to get the greatest income from the least outgo ; and both are justified as single individuals ; but both would be wrong in compelling others to join them by the aid of strikes, societies, unions, &c.

We are told that government should by legislation make such provision for the people as would obviate the necessity of strikes and trades' unions. I protest against this interference by government with our individual affairs. We already have too much of this interference—too much of governmental prying into private business. I am opposed to the whole system as tending to centralization ; to building up a powerful centralized despotism, by the down-pulling of personal rights and individual privileges. If you ask the government to feed, clothe, protect, and furnish you with work, and interpose in your behalf as regards employment and wages, what more natural than for government to turn round and demand from you whatever it chooses in the way of taxes, fat offices, and expensive officials, and a complete surrender of all your personal liberties and individual rights. under the plea of the public good.

No, Mr. Chairman, the workingmen of America should be the very last of all the world to ask protection of government ; but they should be the first to demand of that government the right to be let alone. They should remember that this idea of depending on the government deadens all improvement in their condition. France proves this. There everything has always been done under the fatherly care of the government, and there the condition of the workers has not improved for a hundred years, and never will till the people rise superior to the government. Let American workers ask nothing from the government.

In France, a farmer can neither sow nor reap till the Mayor of the Commune says " do it." And what is their condition ? Non-progressive. And so with all branches of industry in that country : government is all and everything —the workers nobody or nothing.

Keep clear of governmental care ; keep clear of strikes ; shun trades' unions ; keep out of combinations ; stick to individual effort ; make your services so valuable to the employed, so necessary to the public, that they cannot be dispensed with, and you will have no need of strikes or government aid.

HABEAS CORPUS—MARTIAL LAW, &c.

To the Editor of the New York Times:

It occurs to me, Mr. Editor, that all danger of a conflict between the National and State authorities may be avoided by a declaration and en forcement of Martial Law. While such declaration might be in force, there would be no attempts made by county judges to do what honorable and learned judges of the United States Courts would not, in their patriotic wisdom, attempt; or if some notoriety-seeking Justice should be foolish enough to try his powers, he would find a difference between the " say so" of his court and the " do so" of the military authority. A few lessons of this sort would do much toward crushing out Northern sympathy for Southern treason. I am no advocate for National usurpations against State rights. I believe in the rights of the States, and I also believe in the *duty* of the National or United States Government, and one of the most paramount of its duties is the maintenance of its own authority, for on such maintenance depend not only the rights of the States, but also the rights of persons and property. It is not necessary, however, for the Government to declare martial law over the whole State in order to avoid apprehended conflict of authority.

It need only proclaim martial-law to be in force over the places and properties belonging to it, or dock-yards, forts, arsenals, &c., &c. In and over these, the authority and jurisdiction of the Government is supreme, except for the service of civil process by the State authorities, or writs of *habeas corpus*, &c. The right to serve these in these forts and places was reserved to the State when it ceded the lands and water fronts to the Government; but if the Government, in the exercise of its constitutional authority for the upholding of its laws, declares the existence of martial law in and over the places and grounds belonging to it, and adjacent thereto, then the civil law, and the right of the State to serve its processes therein, is for the time suspended, and no good citizen, either on or off the bench, will attempt to interfere. Let martial law be forthwith declared at Fort Lafayette, and all other places where State prisoners are or may be confined.

August 17, 1861.

ABOUT FREEING AND ARMING SLAVES.
[*Anti-Slavery Standard, Aug.* 2, 1862.]

To the President of the United States:

HONORED SIR: If ever the voice of the people might be considered the voice of God, it was when that voice called you to Washington. Partisan politicians had dragged our country down to the lowest deeps of degradation. Conspiracy had poisoned the head of the nation. Treason had mined the foundations of the capital. Volcanoes were rumbling over a great part of our land, threatening to pour forth the lava that should destroy. Dark clouds, portending great storms, appeared on the horizon. Distant thunders, betokening approaching tempests, were heard all around. Fitful gusts of wind gave warning of the coming tornado. The great ship of State, under the control of insane officers and a treason-maddened crew, was rushing on toward deadly breakers. The passengers, wild with affright, and, in their despair, sweating great drops of blood, called for help, and the voice of the ALMIGHTY, spoken by human tongues, called you, ABRAHAM LINCOLN, to the helm. I doubt if sacred or profane history can produce a more direct providential intervention in the affairs of a people. I speak reverently when I say that God knew the instrument he was selecting for the salvation of this nation. I design no flattery for you, Mr. President—none whatever; you are the mere human clay in the hands of the Almighty Potter, to be fashioned by His will. Yet, like all human agents employed by our Universal Father for the good of his children, you are endowed with powers of discretion, and will be held responsible for the proper use thereof. Since you have filled the great office you have been called to, you have done well. I believe no man could have done better. God be praised for what you have accomplished. If the prayers and wishes of thousands of honest hearts are of avail to a public officer, you, Mr. President, have been and are well sustained. Nightly, from the homes of loyal thousands whose loved ones are doing and dying for their country's life, and weekly from ten thousand pulpits, ascend heartfelt prayers for the head of the Nation—for you, Abraham Lincoln. See to it that no deed of yours shall give cause of regret to these prayerful ones. Let not the blessings so lavishly invoked on your head be, by any act of yours, turned to curses. Providence has invested you with as much authority as ever fell to human hands. Use it wisely ; use it well. On assuming this authority, you found your country divided by treason. On the side of the traitors you found slavery ; on the side of loyalty you found freedom. These hosts still oppose each other. Still, slavery is trying to destroy the government established for freedom. Are you doing all that your high position demands for freedom, for government, for right, for justice ? Do you realize, as you ought, that while you hesitate to assume what you may conscientiously consider doubtful powers, in behalf of freedom as against slave-working rebellion, thousands on thousands of your loyal fellow-citizens are going down to their graves ? Do you realize that honest homes are made desolate by camp-engendered disease, that walketh by noonday and resteth not by night ? Death deprived you of a loved one since you have been President—death in its least repulsive form. Your cherished one breathed its last in the arms of parents, surrounded by the care that never tires. Yet you grieved. Think, Mr. President, of the heart-rending miseries that thousands of fathers as loving as yourself daily and hourly suffer by the prolongation of this terrible war. Your child died under your roof; their sons are dying on the battle-fields, wasting in deadly camps, and marching down to the dead from diseased hospitals. Names of killed and wounded and sick fill our papers. Death reaps a rich harvest. Sorrow reigns supreme. Millions of people believe that much, very much, of future woe may be prevented if you will call to the aid of the nation ALL THE HELP within its reach, without stopping to see if the Constitution provides such aid. Our national edifice is on fire. The flames are destroying its timbers. The great want is *water*, WATER. We have no time to waste in discussions as to the nature of these elements. We know that the one that is in the greatest force will conquer. The fire of rebellion, aided by the work done by slaves, is destroying us. Our only safety is in pouring on the WATERS OF FREEDOM fast enough to quench the flames. We have been manning the engines for long, burning months. Our men have dropped dead in their harness. Still we have worked, and still the infernal fire rages. Slaves that are to-day helping rebellion by their labor had rather work for the nation. All they ask is *opportunity*, OPPORTUNITY, OPPORTUNITY. To you, Mr. President, has God intrusted the duty of preserving this nation, of putting out this fire. Will you not rise above all party or personal prejudices, and grasp every and all means that can be reached ? This terrible rebellion is in one section. The other section is loyal. God deals with people in mass. The people of the rebellious States as *a mass* are armed traitors. If there are any loyal States among them, they should be protected in their rights, but such protection should not tend to the defense of traitors nor to the destruction of loyal ones in other States. They may be pitied for the misfortunes of locality. We of the loyal States have suffered, are suffering badly, as *a whole*. This loyal few of the traitor region mustnot complain if they, too, suffer. The nation is rich, is just. If by any act of the government these should sustain unjust loss, they can be made whole—not so with the nation. If its life is taken by this rebellion, no earthly power can restore it. To you, Mr. President, under Providence, we look to preserve its existence. We are laying down our lives and pouring out our money to aid you. All we ask is that we be not utterly exhausted before you call to our assistance the hundreds of thousands of slaves (now working for the rebels), every one of whom would gladly work for us if invited or allowed. As a mass, these slaves are our friends. They have acted as our guides and pilots. They are ready to work and to fight for the old flag, if that flag will only protect them. Justice to them as a people dictates their emancipation. Protection to ourselves demands that we use them. The first principle of war, that of weakening your enemy, requires that we invite them to our lines. Our rebellious enemy lives on the food they produce. His soldiers rest while his slaves do the tiresome work that wears out our brave men. You, Mr. President, can change all this. The common-sense eloquence that your proclamations carry can send hope to the loyal, fear to the rebels, and joy to the slave. As a mass, the people of the rebel States are traitors; as a mass they should be punished, Inviting their slaves to help us would be a punishment: that punishment should be administered. You are the man to apply it. The harvest fields of the loyal States are white with the bread that is to feed us. Hands cannot be had to gather in the great crops a kind Providence has given us. You ask for three hundred thousand more men. The nation is willing to give them. But where shall they come from at this season ? If the harvest is left ungathered, we invite starvation for the future. The rebel States, too, have their harvest to secure. *They have slaves to secure it.* We have none. Thank God we have none. A proclamation from you, Mr. President, inviting their slaves to help us, with a promise of free · dom, would bring more strong arms and willing hearts to our armies in the South than you now ask the loyal States to furnish. This weakens our enemy, gives us the services of men to gather our harvests, and saves the lives of thousands of as true men as ever lived. The wickedness of this treason deserves this punishment. Our own self-preservation demands it. View this in another light. Admit that the majority of the people of the traitor States are loyal and should not be wronged of their property or personal rights. All governments take private property for public uses by paying a reasonable price therefor. Without this well-settled principle nations could not exist. Without it we could have no roads, canals, parks, or other public things. Apply this principle to those loyal ones of the South whose slaves might leave them on your in-vitation. No injustice would ensue. If they are loyal, they ought to aid the nation to the extent of their ability. We of the loyal States do that. Those of the traitor States must bear their share of the burden. This is simple justice. Wherever our army goes, there also go Federal laws. These laws exact obedience from a black slave just as imperatively as from a white freeman. These laws protect the slave in his right to life. For this protection he should yield service. You, Mr. President, can acquire that service. In conclusion, I implore you, by your love of country, by the sympathy you bear your fellow-citizens, by the love of Freedom, by your regard for right, for justice, to call to your aid the help of ALL CLASSES OF PERSONS, IN ALL PARTS OF OUR COUNTRY, whether they be WHITE or BLACK,

BOND OR FREE, NATIVE OR ALIEN, let all who can help have an opportunity, and when in future times the historian writes your name, it will be in LETTERS OF GOLD as the PRESERVER of the NATION. GOD BLESS YOU, ABRAHAM LINCOLN!

CENTRAL REPUBLICAN CLUB.

The Central Republican Club met at room No. 24 Cooper Institute, last evening, Dr. Kennedy in the chair. The meeting was largely attended, and the following resolution, introduced by Mr. Tousey, laid over from last week, was considered:

Resolved, That the surest and quickest way to end the rebellion and establish a permanent peace is to declare immediate and unconditional emancipation.

Mr. Riddle, the first speaker, opposed the adoption of the resolution. He believed there could be no peace except in the preservation of the Union. Our safety was in getting the Union sentiment of the South in active co-operation. The South, if driven to unite against us by a proclamation of emancipation, could never be conquered. Their determined spirit was shown in the expression they had made use of, "that if their mothers were Northern women, they would delight to trample in their blood." Emancipation must needs come, but there was no occasion for hurrying Providence.

Mr. Robert Shannon thought the resolution was just and right, and to the purpose. He was for immediate, unconditional emancipation. Slavery by the South had been made paramount to the Constitution, the Union, and the peace of the country. If we would get rid of our troubles we must get rid of the cause.

Mr. R. M. Poer took the Conservative side. It was a question of expediency. The Abolitionists called expediency cowardice, and it was cowardice, but at the same time necessary. To try to overturn the institution by any sudden shock would involve a war of races, and tear up society by the roots. A lion brought up on milk might be gentle enough to lie down with the lamb, but let that lion once lap blood, and it will be as furious as ever it was in its native wilds. So with the slave when he gets a taste of freedom.

Mr. Tousey said that as Slavery was the cause of the rebellion, of course, if the cause were removed, the effect would cease; he was therefore in favor of the resolution. If, as the Anti-Emancipationists held, the slaves if set free should prove an idle, shiftless, non-producing class, a field would be open for free labor; he was therefore in favor of the resolution. If the Republican party did not adopt the plan of emancipation, the Democratic party would; he would forestall the Democrats; at any rate the party could better afford to be in the right than in the wrong; therefore, he was in favor of the resolution. Loyalty that had to be bought was not worth having, and the Border States would help us but little, without they adopted our cause heart and soul. The rebels were employing the blacks in their army against us, while we would not allow any of our black population to handle a musket or a spade. It seems only necessary that the President should ask people without distinction of color to fight for the Union. He protested against the army receiving fugitives as such. Secretary Cameron had said that if any of the slaves desired to go back to their masters, why, don't "hinder them." But this was only opening the door for spies. If the people of England—he did not refer to the aristocracy—believed we were fighting for freedom, we should get their sympathy. If the South had the right to hold slaves under the Constitution, that right was now abrogated by her violation of that instrument. For these and other reasons the speaker favored the resolution.

Mr. Walker also spoke for the resolution. Not a drop of blood was shed in the West Indies on the occasion of emancipation. In 1848, when the French abolished slavery, not a drop of blood was shed by negroes. He referred to an article in *The Westminster Review*, showing that in pounds, shillings, and pence emancipation was a benefit to the West Indies and to Great Britain herself.

Mr. Wm. Oland Bourne offered a resolution as a substitute to the one before the meeting, taking the ground that in the present condition of the country there can be but two parties, one maintaining inviolate the Constitution and the Union, and the Government established by it; and the other, directly with arms, or indirectly by other means, conspiring to overthrow the Constitution and destroy the Union and the Government. To pass the first resolution would be to stultify Congress, the Republican party, and the Constitution itself. He referred to the resolutions of the 23d of July, which declared that the war was for the preservation of the Government, and not one of oppression. He also read an article from the *Tribune* of June 5, 1861, in regard to the effect of the war.

At the conclusion of Mr. Bourne's remark, without taking any action on the resolutions, the Club adjourned for one week.

N. Y. Tribune, August 28, 1861.

[This organization was the first one in the Union to discuss Emancipation by the national authorities. The discussion continued for several weeks and excited much attention, both at home and abroad.]

" BARBARITIES OF THE WAR."

To the Editor of the New York Times:

Your remarks under the above head, in Thursday's issue, were very good ; but do not, in my opinion, reach the case. You attribute the barbaric atrocities wreaked on our poor soldiers, to the Proclamation of Davis and Beauregard. *Incidentally,* this may be true. *Primarily,* it is short of the truth. The cause of these outrages is nothing more nor less than the inherent and natural *barbarism of Slavery.* No slaveholder is or can be civilized. They may be highly educated—many are—but the most refined and intelligent are simply *educated barbarians*—nothing more, nothing less. Slavery is an aggression on the rights of others, founded on force over weakness—the invariable practice of all barbarians—and those who practice Slavery know nothing of civilization and the amenities of that kind of society. Davis and Beauregard merely gave wordy forms,' in their Proclamations, to the barbarism of their slaveholding habits, and these Proclamations would have been like seed on dry ground, but for the institution of Slavery existing among and upheld by those to whom these proclamations were addressed. This institution had, by its barbaric tendencies, fitted the ground to receive the terrible seed sown by the rebel leaders in their proclamations. These men are by nature no worse nor more savage than we of the North, but Slavery has made them barbarians, and compelled them to be what they are. They will always be cruel to their opponents as long as they are unjust enough to be slaveholders. Where there is no Slavery among educated people there will be none of these barbarities. Abolish Slavery, and these men become civilized, and these atrocities will cease and the rebellion be crushed. Slavery is barbarism, and those who practice it are only barbarians and must be cruel to all who oppose them. Yours, &c.

August, 1861.

ABOUT PRISONERS OF WAR, PRIVATEERS, &c.

To the Editor of the New York Times :

In your paper of last Thursday, you seem to have some hesitancy as to the proper way of treating prisoners of war, pirates and others found in arms against the government and people of the United States. Do not accuse me of egotism if I assert that there is no need of any halting (but there is need of a vast amount of haltering) in the matter. What are the facts ? A part of the people have attempted to subvert the government by force of arms. The government (the centralized and legal embodiment of the people), in maintaining its authority, also resorts to arms. Collisions and battles occur. Both sides take prisoners. Now comes the question, " What shall be done with these men ?" I admit the question is one of vast importance, not only as regards the proper way of dealing with the rebellion, but also as to the *personal* rights and privileges, pains and penalties of the captured men. *The government should not treat its captured rebels as prisoners of war.* Neither should it do that other and much worse thing, discharge them on their parol. To do the first is a virtual admission that the rebels are a *lawful enemy*. This must not be admitted. If it is, ground is laid for their recognition by foreign nations. The government must do all in its power to place the rebels *outside* of law, and not allow them to claim or exercise any legal privileges whatever.

They are rebels, and should be treated as such. When taken in arms against the government, they should be disarmed, and compelled to aid the government in maintaining itself against the rebels. They should never be treated as prisoners of war, neither should the government ever recognize a flag of truce from rebels. Every man bearing such a flag should be arrested as a rebel, the bearing the flag being *prima facie* evidence of his being a rebel ; for if there were no rebels there could be no rebellion, and if there were no rebellion, there would be no war or collision needing the intercession of a flag of truce. Every bearer of one should be locked up as a rebel. No treating with them as lawful enemies. No discharging or swearing allegiance. Men that forswear their natural inherited allegiance, by engaging in a rebellion against a government like ours, cannot be trusted on their oath, especially an oath taken under such circumstances. Never trust a rebel's oath.

So much for land rebels. Now about rebels and pirates afloat. They should be hung at the yard-arm of the national vessel capturing them, without ever being brought ashore to be tried and sympathized with, and kept at the public expense. The summary hanging of a few would scare the rest and drive them from the ocean. It may be asked, why hang water rebels (pirates), and not hang land rebels ? I answer, the former not only rebel against and defy the Government, but add to that the preying on *private property*, and by all laws of all nations are outlaws, and not entitled to any of the legal amenities of ordinary criminals. The excuse that they have letters-of-marque from the head rebel is of no avail. He cannot delegate power to others that he does not hold himself. He and his rebel coadjutors have no legal national existence, and their warrants for piracy (or privateering) are of no more validity than so much paper from a wild Comanche chief, authorizing raids on the border settlers. All these piratical rebels should be hung at the yard-arm instanter. Being caught in the act is proof enough without wasting time in court trials. If they are not pirates then is TILLMAN a murderer, and should be given over to trial and execution. I may be told that if we hang these men, the rebels will retaliate on our men taken by them. In fact, this is already threatened. Well, terrible as it is, the sentence must be written. *Let them retaliate.* Do not accuse me of barbarism or lack of sympathy for our poor unfortunates who are now or may hereafter be prisoners. I have personal friends now in their hands, and realize fully what I write when I say "let the rebels retaliate". If we hesitate one moment to hang their pirates and punish their rebels on account of any fear for the safety of our men in their hands, or in consequence of any threats they make, then we may just as well lay down our arms and yield up the government to them, and sue for mercy.

Rebels taken in arms against the government must not be treated as prisoners of war subject to an exchange. To do so discourages our own loyal men, who will not fight for such result. Flags of truce borne by rebels must not be respected, but their bearers must be treated as rebels. To do otherwise is to encourage treason. Privateers must be summarily hanged as a warning to others and as a protection to law-abiding citizens. No leniency, no recognition of letters-of-marque, no attention to threats of retaliation. Let the Government be firm, and swift in its punishment of treason and piracy, and peace will the sooner return to our borders.

August, 1861.

[*From the Knickerbocker Magazine, October*, 1861.]
(Written in August, 1861.)
EMANCIPATION.
ITS INFLUENCE ON THE REBELLION AND EFFECT ON THE WHITES.

WE are in a rebellion or insurrection of extraordinary magnitude. Common consent attributes it to the existence of Slavery. The cause being removed, the disease dies. The removal of a dam allows the free course of the stream. Remove the dam of Slavery from the broad river of the Union, and the pure waters of Freedom will speedily wash this foul scum of Rebellion into the great gulf of the Past. Slavery, however, is, in the opinion of many well-meaning people, a *constitutional* disease, to be removed only by a remodeling of that instrument to suit the new condition of the political patient. The honest scruples of these persons must be respected. Another large class assert that the disease is not constitutional, but in violation of that law of national life, and that all our political diseases arise from such violation. The opinions of these people are also entitled to attention, and however they may differ from the former on these matters, all agree that, had there been no slavery in the South, there would have been no rebellious attempts to overthrow the Government and extend "the institution." This is the common platform on which all stand, one of its planks being a desire to end this rebellion and establish peace with honor to the Government and the people. So far so good.

Another plank in this political structure is the admission that Emancipation would end the rebellion at once and effectually. The first-named parties, that is to say, those who believe that the Constitution protects Slavery, are loth to adopt this course so long as there is any possibility of otherwise crushing the rebellion, but are willing to resort to this remedy if nothing else will cure the disease. I would willingly address a few words to this class. Many of the wisest and best men whom our country has ever produced, deny most emphatically that the Constitution protects or even recognizes Slavery, but for the present purpose let it be admitted that it does both recognize and protect that institution. Now it is a principle of law, as well as of common sense and common justice that those who violate the law do by such acts forfeit their rights to enjoy the privileges the law guarantees to those who obey its provisions. Thus, murderers, burglars, forgers, or any criminals who transgress the law, forfeit their rights under it, and are deprived of their liberties, or it may be of their lives, simply because they have done unpardonable violence to the law; and any attorney who should set up the plea that his murdering or thieving client was having his legal rights interfered with by the gallows or the prison, would naturally deserve and gain the contempt of the community. Violators of law forfeit their claims to the rights guaranteed to those who obey it. If such violators continued to enjoy the same privileges in society as those who never offend, there would be an end to all law, and civilization be extinguished. Force would take the place of order, and the weak yield to the strong.

The distinguishing trait of civilization is, that the weakest member of the community is, in the eye of the law, strong as the strongest ; were it otherwise, there could be no civilization. The South, or those living in the Southern States, *who have by their rebellion violated the Constitution,*

2

have forfeited their claims to its protection, and are now, in their relation to the government, in the same position as that of a convicted criminal towards society—they have no legal or constitutional rights left them except the right of trial, and that trial is now going on from day to day in presence of the whole world, having DEITY for the presiding Judge and humanity for the jury, and must be dealt with by government as the law and society deal with individual criminals. They must be *punished* for their transgressions, and as these have been greater than the transgressions of any single criminal, so the punishment to be awarded must be great in proportion, and the severest that can be inflicted is to deprive them of that institution for the perpetuation of which, as their so-styled Vice-President declares, they began the rebellion. Hence we may assume that it will be right, proper, and efficacious to proclaim Emancipation throughout the rebellious States, and that such declaration will not, for the reasons above given, be any violation of the Constitution or any infringement of their legal rights.

There are many who admit the efficacy of Emancipation, but who—timid and temporizing—invariably speak of it as a " last resort." And why *last ?* It is admitted that this rebellion is purely and solely the work cf the slaveholders. It is also admitted that the government would be justified in proclaiming Emancipation "*as a last resort.*" Allow me to ask what is meant by this " *last resort ?*" If it is meant that when the government, backed up by the people of the loyal States, shall have tried by other means to crush this rebellion, and failing in all others, then, and not till then, Emancipation is to be proclaimed—if this is what is meant by a " *last resort,*" allow me to suggest that it is a most " lame and impotent conclusion." Think. It is proposed to have government do all it can by its armies, by blockade, by non-intercourse, by stopping mails, by fines, by imprisonment, etc., and failing with all these powerful aids to crush the most wicked rebellion that ever cursed humanity,·then Emancipation may be proclaimed. The proclamations of a government thus defeated in its attempts to maintain its existence by putting down such a rebellion, would not be worth the paper they were written on. *Who would respect them ?* Not those whom its armies could not conquer ; not those whom its fines and imprisonment could not intimidate ; not those whom it would, by proclamation, liberate. Why ? Because a government thus weak, thus unable to maintain itself by enforcing its laws, would not have the power to make its proclamations respected. If such a proclamation is to be issued at all, now is the time, while the government is strong, or has the credit of being strong enough to make its proclamations respected.

Thus much for the scruples of the temporizers, and their willingness to use Emancipation as a "last resort." Let us now discuss a side-issue, and one that is often urged as an objection to Emancipation. I refer to the fear that a declaration of Emancipation would inaugurate a servile insurrection, and that a second act of the St. Domingo tragedy would be enacted in our Southern States. But why should the slaves join in insurrection, and cut their masters' throats, *in face of the fact, that the government had proclaimed Emancipation, and would in self-defense enforce such proclamation by its armies,* just as it does and must enforce all its other acts? The government having proclaimed these slaves free, they then become men, would be no longer "chattels personal;" and being men, would be entitled to the rights of citizens, and consequently to protection from government. In enforcing this protection, government might use these freed people themselves as instruments with which to execute its decrees, while at the same time this very use of them *implies the ability of government to control them, and thus most effectually prevent all possibility of servile insurrections on the part of the blacks,* as it is now trying to do with the more dangerous insurrection of their white masters. The true and only way forever to prevent all slave insurrections is to have no slaves to rise.

There were no unusual or improper excitements when Emancipation took effect in the British West Indies. There would be none here. As the hour drew near that was to set thousands of human beings free, and transform them from mere chattels to human beings, every breath grew shorter, every pulse beat quicker, and every ear listened with intense eagerness to catch the first sound of that bell that was to proclaim "Liberty throughout all the Land unto all the inhabitants thereof," and when its last echoes died away in the valley of those beautiful islands, there arose such a shout of joy as never before found vent from human lips. So would it be in our own South. Emancipation never begot insurrection. That is the natural offspring of Slavery.

I have thus disposed of the Insurrectionary objections, and will now consider the *conceded* rights of loyal slaveholders in the rebellious States, for it is admitted that they have rights which should be respected. Let government lay a tax on the whole people of the Confederacy, loyal and rebellious, and collect it, when laid, at the point of the bayonet if necessary (and this, as a matter of pecuniary economy, would be better than to carry on a long war), and pay these loyal men for their slaves. Let the same be done with the border slave States, and thus by purchase from good citizens and by confiscation from rebellious ones, would be established Universal Emancipation throughout our United States.

I have thus argued the case up to the establishment of Emancipation. I will now consider its influence as a means of crushing the rebellion. Facts warrant the assumption, that this rebellion had its origin in, and is carried on for the sole purpose of extending and perpetuating slavery. All the orators of the South, all the leaders of their public opinion, take this position ; they even say that our present Constitution is good enough in every particular save one, and that one defect in that great document is, that it does not provide sufficiently for the extension, perpetuation, and protection of slavery, and therefore, as they have not at the present time the *political power* to alter that instrument (in accordance with its provisions) so as to suit it to their views, they resort to *physical force*, and cover their States with great armies, with the avowed determination of destroying this Constitution and the government founded on it, and thus making room for their own more perfect *Slavery-making, bondage-extending document*. This is their avowed object, patent to the world. Now, if we can, by any means proper to use, put an end to this institution, will not such act put an end to this wicked rebellion ? If we effectually extinguish slavery in the rebellious States, and prohibit its future introduction there, will we not establish peace ? If cause precedes effect, we will most assuredly. The rebels must lay down their arms and submit to the laws when we have deprived them of the power (I assume that we have the power to enforce our proclamation, and if we have not, we are no longer a government) to continue the existence of their institution, and thus we shall see the positive influence of Emancipation as a means to crush the rebellion and establish peace. Let Emancipation be proclaimed, and down goes the Slaveholders' Rebellion.

Having thus established the position that Emancipation will crush out the insurrection, I will now consider its effects on the whites of both sections, South as well as North. I assume that there is a certain amount of labor to be done in the Southern States, and that the freed negroes, from experience and acclimation, are the best qualified persons to perform that labor, and would be employed to do it under a system of wages (instead of the lash), prices being regulated by the laws of demand and supply. These negroes, being thus paid for their work, would consume more of the products of white men employed in the mechanic arts ; more especially those products not absolutely necessary to life, as cheap ornaments, and those thousands of fancy articles that an uneducated people are so fond of, and which they always buy so freely in proportion to heir means. But, it may be said, this system of wages would enhance the cost of the products grown by the labor of these people, and this increased cost would have to be borne by the consumers of these products.

If this were true, it would be owing to the fact, that these black people free would get more for their labor than black people in bondage ; and if this were so, then it would follow, that the freeing of these people would have the effect of "*leveling up*" the price of labor to a point where the poor white men of those regions could afford to do it, a condition of things not heretofore existing in any slave State, the rule there being, that the planter, who owns both capital and labor, can afford to do work cheaper than the poor white, who merely owns his labor, which he wishes to sell, and can find no market for, because he cannot work as cheap as the black slave of the capitalist. Hence it is, that there are so many of the " poor white trash" scattered all over the South. Emancipation, according to this reasoning (originated by the opponents of Emancipation), would benefit the poor white most decidedly. The increased demand by the freed blacks for the products of the whites, both South and North, would add greatly to the demand for the labor of these whites, and thus Emancipation would benefit them pecuniarily, to say nothing of its removing the degradation now attached to labor in consequence of slavery. Where there are no slaves, laboring men are respectable and respected. Where slavery exists, the laborer is neither. The New England States illustrate the one condition, and the South the others But, say some, if you emancipate the negroes they will not work ; the stimulus of wages is not sufficient to induce them to labor. Well, grant that they will not. Suppose they choose to drag out a miserable, hand-to-mouth existence, as the poor whites of the South now do, and earn barely enough under the pressure of starvation to support life. What, then ? If they refuse to work as regularly and efficiently as heretofore, will not *their refusal make a demand for the labor of the poor whites of both sections, and thus materially help to draw off from the great cities of the North the surplus labor, now vainly seeking employment, and thus greatly benefit those laborers ?* Such neglect to work by the freed negroes would have none other than a beneficial effect on the poor whites, by giving them the work that the free blacks refuse to do ; but if the freed blacks go on and work industriously for wages, then their increased ability to consume would of necessity make an increased demand for the products of white men, now employed in the manufactures consumed by the blacks. Thus Emancipation, like all GOOD DEEDS, would bring its own reward.

I have thus endeavored to show that a proclamation of Emancipation would end the rebellion ; that its effects would be beneficial to the whites, and if my arguments are sound, let the People, who make and unmake administrations, demand of the present Government an immediate PROCLAMATION OF EMANCIPATION.

[The above article was written in August, just before the appearance of Fremont's Proclamation. Its appearance in an old conservative magazine like the Knickerbocker, caused considerable excitement amongst its readers, many of whom banished it from their libraries; nevertheless, that particular number met a much larger s le than usual.]

[*The following appeared in the New York daily papers, in January,* 1862.]

OBJECTIONS TO THE PROPOSED STAMP TAX ON NEWSPAPERS, MAGAZINES, AND OTHER PERIODICALS.

I am opposed to this proposition in toto. It is bad in theory, and worse in practice. Why? The present prices of newspapers, &c., will not admit of the proposed duty being paid by the publishers. If the tax is paid by them, its cost must be added to the price paid by the consumer. This must curtail their sale and circulation. This curtailment of sale injures all industries connected with the manufacture of the paper—such as papermakers, binders, engravers, printers, pressmen, inkmakers, expressmen, &c.

Government should do nothing to cripple the legitimate manufactures of its people. The proposed tax or stamp duty would thus cripple an important industry, besides requiring more capital to conduct the business than is now required.

Why more capital? The duty to be collected by stamping each copy or sheet published would require the printing of the stamp in some Government office, or under the supervision of some Government official, *before the publisher could use it* for printing his matter thereon; and this requires an increased amount of unprinted paper to be kept on hand. Again, the money for the stamp must be paid to the Government before the publisher sells and gets pay for his paper; and this is another addition to the capital required for publishing papers, &c. This shuts men of limited means out of the business, by requiring heavy capital to conduct it.

Government should not, by its legislation, discourage legitimate trade of any kind, by any system of special taxation that would require additional capital to conduct such trade. The true interest of the people is best promoted by that sort of legislation that leaves the people free to engage in any and as many different callings as their inclinations prompt and their capital will admit. Onerous taxes on specified articles are sure to cripple such industries. The proposed stamp-tax is one of this kind, and ought never to be laid.

Again, Government should do all in its power to promote the spread of intelligence and knowledge among its people. Its own greatness is promoted thereby; its own permanence is guaranteed by this course. The strength of the Government depends more on the intelligent minds of its people than on the muscles of their arms. Proof of this: The greatest number of papers, &c., read in America, are read in the Free States; the fewest in the Slave States. The former are all loyal and true to the Government; all of them responded with alacrity to the calls of the Executive for men and money. Nearly all of the latter are in rebellion against the Government, and some of those few which are not, set up the plea of neutrality, or refused to furnish men for the Union until their own borders were invaded by rebel troops. Had there been as many low-priced, largely circulated, well-conducted papers in the Slave States as in the Free, it would have been impossible to have gotten up the present rebellion. Good government depends on intelligence. Despotism rests on ignorance. Any tax that adds to the price of paper, &c., containing intelligence for the people, restricts the spread of that intelligence, and that hurts the Government.

A case in point : Government desires to inform its citizens of the proceedings of Congress. Why ? That they may be the better able to know what their representatives and Executive are doing. To this end Congress allows the *Congressional Globe* to go through the mails everywhere *free of postage.* If the dissemination of the information contained in the *Globe* is of no benefit to the people, why let it go *post free?* Every person knows, and the Government through Congress admits, that this information is of vital interest to all, and therefore Congress wisely allows all newspapers sent to publishers in exchange for others to pass through the mails free of postage. Why ? The better to enable each publisher to fill his paper with the greatest amount of information for the people. Congress acts wisely in this. Again, Congress is now discussing, or has passed a bill fixing the postage on public documents at two cents a pound, while the postage on other printed matter is sixteen cents a pound. Why this difference? Because Congress considers that the dissemination of the information contained in those documents is important to the people. This is right. There should be no special tax on knowledge.

If Congress wants to raise money by taxation, let it be done by a general and uniform tax on the entire property or capital of the country, of every kind and nature, and not on any particular industry that adds to that property and capital.

Perhaps there is no country in the world that has so few persons unable to read, in proportion to the entire population, as our own, and this universal ability to read is traceable, in a great degree, to the cheapness with which the ability to read can be made useful by means of an unrestricted and cheap press; for of what use would the art of reading be to the mass of poor people if the price of books, papers, &c., &c., were beyond their reach ? The productions of the low-priced periodical press have done as much to instruct the people as have our schools. In fact but for the cheapness of reading matter furnished by the periodical press much of the rudimentary learning taught in these schools would have been limited in its usefulness. The periodical press, being left free and unrestricted by governmental interference—free from all offensive taxation, free as other branches of industry from special imposts---has reached a sphere of universal usefulness never before known, and to restrict that usefulness now by a stamp-tax, or impost duty on its production, is to set back progress, and require the people to dispense with one of the most potent agencies for the dissemination of universal intelligence that their wants demanded or ingenuity could produce. A stamp-tax on newspapers and other periodicals destroys the power of this agency just in proportion as that tax adds to the cost of the paper thus taxed by curtailing its sale.

The great cheapness of the newspaper press of America has given it its enormous circulation. This unparalleled circulation has given it the very great influence it wields. This influence is caused by the principles inculcated, by the ideas discussed, by the information conveyed, by the vast amount of knowledge laid before the people through its columns. Any special tax or stamp duty laid on the press lessens this influence, retards the spread of intelligence, and injures the whole community.

For example : Either one of our city dailies contains each morning a perfect epitome of the world's history for the previous twenty-four hours. With this history go forth to millions of readers the thoughts, acts, principles, ideas of the world's great minds—beacons that light mankind along the stormy coasts of life. These papers contain enough to make a good sized volume, and are sold for the very low price of two cents (at most) per copy. This comparatively low price gives them their enormous circulation by placing them within the reach of nearly the entire reading community. Had their price been greater they would never have obtained their present circulation. Their higher-priced predecessors never circulated more hundreds than these now do thousands, and their columns were in their time as satisfactory to their patrons as are the columns of the present dailies to theirs. Nothing but the low price of the latter gave them their circulation, and nothing but the high price of the former caused their limited sale and final discontinuance. Connected with the vast circulation of the cheap press are the interests of all who advertise other branches of trade in their columns. Many manufacturers have derived great benefits from the increased demand caused by their wares being made known to consumers by advertising. Any curtailment of circulation hurts these advertising manufacturers and tradesmen. Any tax or impost duty on newspapers advances the price thereof, and this curtails circulation. Every person is benefited by a cheap press. Everybody is injured by hampering it with onerous taxes.

It is proposed to levy a quarter or half cent per copy on all newspapers published. Now, as I have before stated, the publishers cannot afford to pay either of these sums without increasing the price to the consumer; and as we have no coin in circulation of less value than one cent, the price of the paper paying this tax must be advanced one full cent per copy, and this increased price will cause a very great curtailment in their sale; in fact, would kill off three-fourths of all the papers in the Union. An extra cent per copy may seem to be but a small matter to some persons, but it is quite enough to act as an embargo on the sales of newspapers. It is not only this one cent extra on one single paper, but it is multiplied by fifty-two in a year, if on a weekly, and three hundred and twelve times on a daily, a very serious matter to the purchaser whose means are limited, and quite sufficient to cause them to "stop the paper" in these hard times.

Let the press be as free as possible. Let it be free from onerous taxation, and left unfettered by special duties to do its just work.

[This bill did not become a law.]

[*The following appeared in the New York daily papers in January,* 1862.]

THE EXPRESS SYSTEM.

The following are the principal objections, forcibly stated, to Mr. Colfax's new bill in relation to transporting newspapers outside of the mails. They are from the pen of Mr. Tousey, of the firm of Ross & Tousey, and sufficiently expose the errors in Mr. Colfax's impracticable scheme:

"This bill makes it unlawful for any person to carry any newspapers over any post-route out of the mails. I object to this as interfering with the purchase and sale of merchandise by restricting the free transportation thereof. Newspapers, magazines and other printed matter are as much articles of merchandise, as are drygoods, groceries, hardware or any other thing that enters into the consumption of the people, and should be subjected to no more hindrances in sale and transportation than they are. It is the duty of government to encourage the production and consumption of home manufactured articles, not to restrict such production, and if revenue be the object, let taxes be laid on the capital invested in and produced by the profits of manufacturing, whether such profits are made from the production of hats, boots, clothing, or newspapers and books. The free and expeditious system of transporting printed matter outside of the mails that is now in practice, is one of the most potent agents for the dissemination of knowledge among the people that has ever been devised, and is the result of long experience, prompted by the inability of the mail or post-office system to meet the emergencies of the case. From this system has grown the vast increase in the circulation of daily and weekly papers, magazines, &c., &c., and from this increased sale and circulation has grown a demand for a great amount of labor to produce the presses to print these papers, for the paper on which they are printed, the ink they are printed with, machinery for the manufacture of the paper, for the production of twine, for the use of carts, wagons, &c.; in fact, there is scarcely a branch of industry that has not been affected beneficially by the increased sale and circulation of printed matter outside of the mails; and to interfere with these interests is to cause a great wrong to all concerned, with no benefit to the Department. The true duty of the government is to let the people devise their own modes of transportation of their merchandise, leaving them free, however, to use such facilities as government provides for transporting other matter, without compelling them, under fine and penalty, to use such facilities.

The government claims the right to manage the transportation of the *written correspondence* of the country. This requires certain machinery. Now, if the people choose to send their PRINTED matter through these channels, under such rules and at such prices as the government makes and demands, they should be left free to do so; but to compel them to send all their newspapers, magazines, and other periodicals that way is an interference with the rights of the people that cannot be justified on any ground whatever. If government thus interferes with the transportation of printed matter, it will be reasonable to expect it will next interfere with the transportation of all kinds of merchandise, and then follows a long list of government officials for the enforcement of the rules and collection of the tariffs demanded by the law, and from this restriction in transportation arises an increase of price ; this lessens production, and thus all branches of labor are affected, and thus government itself is made the loser by the curtailment of wealth or capital on which to levy taxes. The interest of all, both people and government, is best promoted by leaving the people to take care of their own interests. A single illustration of my position is all I will make at this time, and no one knows its truth better than Mr. Colfax. It is this : The present rates of letter postage, based on weight, has been and is the cause of an unheard-of increase in the manufacture of paper, envelopes, and the thousand branches of trade connected with their production, giving employment to thousands of persons, who, but for this labor, would be seeking work in other branches, to the detriment of other workers. The present system of transporting printed matter outside of the mails has also given labor to thousands of persons, who, but for this, would now be crowding other and overstocked labor markets. The bill proposes the granting of licenses by the Postmaster-General. Now, if there is any one thing more than another that the people of this country detest, it is the license system. It is one of the most despised relics of a bygone system of governmental espionage that was always condemned by every people, and by none more than by our own. We have none too great a respect for the necessary and proper officers of the government, such as tax-gatherers, customs officers, and the like, who have no license for special purposes, or for private profit ; and when it is proposed to create a most odious monopoly, as this bill does, and then license special persons to make a profit out of that monopoly, the system of license becomes utterly abhorrent, and must beget the most intense hatred of the system, and a determination to evade its requirements. The true theory of government is to have as few laws as possible, and have those such as will command the respect and voluntary obedience of its people ; not to burden them with odious enactments that they will be sure to revolt against. No more hated officer could be devised than one having a license to use a monopoly for his own selfish ends, and the license proposed in this bill is one of that class.

Perhaps Mr. Colfax thinks that there would be no profit attached to the license. If there is no profit to and from it, then no one will take it, and no income will accrue to the department by its establishment ; and if no one can be found to take it, Mr. C. must do one of two things : Either he will restrict the transportation of printed matter to the mails, or he must appoint some person to superintend its transportation outside, and this involves an increased expenditure by the department ; in either case an increased rate of transportation will ensue, which must cripple the sale of papers. But to come back to the license. Suppose a license to be given or sold to Jones, a news agent, authorizing him to transport printed matter outside of the mails between New York city and Boston, or any other points.

Suppose, further, that Mr. Smith is a wholesale news dealer, residing in New York, and has a customer in New Haven, or any other city or village (on the line of Mr. Jones' licensed route), sent on the supplies with the same sort of paper that Mr. Jones is licensed to carry. Now, the customer of Smith must have his papers at the very earliest moment after the train arrives at his place, and if Jones, licensed by the Postmaster-General, can deliver his papers to him three, five, ten, or fifteen minutes sooner outside of the mails than Smith's customer can get them through the mail, then Smith loses his trade, and Jones gets it. In the receipt and sale of newspapers time is everything to the seller, and minutes represent dollars. Again, if Smith, the wholesale dealer, is compelled to send his papers through the mails to his country customers, and Jones is permitted by his license to carry his outside, he can, in nine cases out of ten, deliver the daily papers to his country customers when Smith's customer would get none, *from the fact* that the time that Smith occupies in getting his papers ready for the mail and the time used in getting them to the post-office to be assorted and bagged, and the further time required to transport them from the post-office to the depot or boat for transportation, is just so much time gained by Jones, the licentiate, to get ahead of Smith, who is just as active as Jones, and would never be behind him, but for being compelled to use the mails, while Jones is not. Let me explain this to those unacquainted with the very peculiar nature of the business which this bill proposes to change. There are in New York, Philadelphia, Baltimore, Boston, and other cities, large establishments, whose business it is to take daily and other newspapers from the offices of publication, and pack all the different papers in one parcel that may be taken by a retailer living out of these cities. These parcels are all conveyed together to the place of shipment, and forwarded by express, or by some special person, whose business it is to see to their delivery at destination. Many of these parcels are thrown from the trains while in motion—that is, thrown off at places where the trains do not stop. Now, it is of daily occurrence that but a few minutes transpire between the time these papers are printed and the departure of the trains or boats—in fact, I have known but half an hour allowed for bringing in some twenty thousand papers, counting them out among some one hundred and fifty different parcels, tying up those parcels, and carting them nearly a mile to the place of shipment.

It is, therefore, easily seen that any hindrance or delay in getting these parcels ready for transportation must seriously affect all concerned, and more especially must that party be injured who is compelled to use the mails, while another party is allowed, under a license, to transport all his papers outside. A monopoly of this kind in the hands of a licentiate will virtually give that party the whole of the business on the line of his route. Perhaps Mr. Colfax may say that the paper must be printed at such hours as suits the departure of the mails. No; Mr. C. will not say that, for he is a publisher, and knows that the publishers of daily papers must, especially in these times, delay going to press till the very latest moment, in order to get the last item of news that is "clicked" over the wires. Perhaps Mr. Colfax will say that his licentiate will be compelled to carry parcels of papers for every person that desires to send. That does not appear in the bill; in fact, the bill, in its spirit, will not allow of any such construction. It prohibits certain things except under license. That license implies certain privileges to be enjoyed by the licentiate. That implies, and in fact is, a monopoly, and that monopoly redounds to the advantage of the licentiate, who, in this case, can force every person to deal with him, or be behind-hand with articles whose only value depends on being up to time. Monopolies of this kind are the most odious and untenable of all. This system will enable an unscrupulous licentiate to refuse to transport whatever he pleases to prohibit. I may be told that the regulations to be established by the Postmaster-General will provide against all this. Then I protest against placing any such authority in his hands, for that office may be filled by an unscrupulous partisan or bigoted sectarian, who could, under this bill, easily favor the periodicals he approved, and retard the distribution of those he disliked. We have already had too much of official tampering with the mails; too much of official and uncontrolled censorship of newspaper transportation in the mails; too much of throwing out or entirely suppressing such papers as did not please the views of the local postmasters; too much interference with the sale and circulation of northern papers in the Southern States. True, these interferences and censorships have been illegal and sectional. Let them continue thus unlawful and sectional, and not attempt to make them lawful and national by vesting any unnecessary authority in the hands of any one—not even in the hands of a Postmaster-General or his licensed subordinates. The system is bad every way; it has not one redeeming trait to recommend it. Let it be rejected. The only true plan for the Government to adopt in relation to the mails and mail routes is to make them free to be used by all on the same terms, without licenses, and make them as secure from any violation as life itself, leaving the people at liberty to use them if they choose, or seek such other modes for transporting their printed matter as best suits them. Perhaps Mr. Colfax expects to increase the revenues of the Post-office Department by compelling all printed matter to go in the mails or pay license for going over post routes outside. In this I think he will be mistaken as he must see that those transporting the mails will have to be paid largely increased prices for mail service, as those parties, railroads, steamboats, &c., now derive large incomes from the transportation of this matter outside of the mails, which income would be cut off by this bill, and a greatly increased amount of mail service required of them, which deficiency of income and increased service must be paid for by the Department. To this increased cost of mail service Mr. Colfax will have to add the cost of labels, stamps, the pay of agents or clerks to see to the whole matter, and the endless string of costly items attending the whole thing, so that when the balance is struck, but little, if anything, would accrue to his revenues —much less than the community would lose by the curtailed business of those interested in the manufacture, distribution and sale of the papers and magazines, and other periodicals Mr. Colfax proposes to tax by this bill. The scheme is not feasible, and should be abandoned. There is no more reason in thus taxing the transportation of newspapers consumed by people living away from the places of their publication, than there is for taxing the carriage of those consumed by people living in those places, and surely Mr. Colfax is not prepared to levy a tax on papers delivered by carriers to people living at or near the place of publication. If revenue is the aim, a better way is to require publishers to pay a stamp duty or tax on every copy they publish, and when that tax or stamp is paid, then leave the buyer and consumer free to transport the paper in any way that best suits them. This plan, objectionable as it is to all our past history, abhorrent as it is to the spirit and genius of our institutions, is far preferable to the prohibitions and licensed monopolies proposed by this bill.

In these times our people desire to know what is going on, and the success of our Government, and stability of our laws, and existence as a nation, is best promoted by disseminating as rapidly, as freely, and as cheaply as possible, all kinds of intelligence among them. The government itself is largely interested in this, more especially when it requires men or money. A largely circulated paper carries to the people all the requisitions of the Government for troops, informs them of its financial needs, and by this universal spread of information, it is enabled to have prompt and speedy responses to its requirements. A crippled press cripples the Government—a universally circulated press helps the Government, by informing the people of its wants. There should be no restrictions placed in the way of the press. Government should do all in its power to extend intelligence. Let this bill be " postponed indefinitely."

[The bill referred to did not pass Congress.]

CONFISCATION OF SLAVES—JUSTICE OR VINDICTIVENESS.

To the editor of the New York Times :

I clip the following extract from your columns of the January 24th, 1862:

> " Another bill, authorizing the President to emancipate the slaves of rebel owners, was then discussed and tabled by a vote equally decided. It is evident the House hesitates to enter on this vindictive business."

You claim to be a loyal man. I believe you are, yet the last sentence of the above extract might be construed otherwise. Let us see. The Government is at war for its existence. Its foes are its own children. Those children do all in their power to destroy their parent. They have, among others, one peculiar source of strength that enables them to place more men under arms against the Government than they could, but for this source. It is proposed to deprive these rebellious children of this source of strength and place it on the side of the Government, and you style this proposition " vindictive." It is a new idea that in war a measure tending to weaken your enemy is vindictive. War means destruction. To destroy your enemy is not vindictive. If he has a vulnerable point you are bound, in justice to those who fight your battles, to assail him in that point, and doing so is not vindictive. The labor performed by the slaves of the rebels would have to be performed by their soldiers if their slaves were taken from them. This would weaken them just so much. In the rebel States there are slaves sufficient to do the work of as many white men as are now in the rebel army. Deprive these rebels of their slaves and you destroy their armies, either by forcing them to become working producers, or by starvation arising from non-production. Either way destroys your enemy, by lessening his strength. But, say you, the residents of the rebel States are not *all rebels*. Granted ; still, that does not affect the proposition which proposes to take *only* the slaves of rebels. But, you ask, how will we discriminate between the rebels and those who are loyal? Thus: We will confiscate every slave in the rebellious States and invite them to come to our side. If it is found that in this general confiscation the slaves of really true and loyal men have been made free, we will pay for their ransom at a reasonable rate. But, say you, this is an interference with the rights of the States, as slavery is a State institution, and not to be meddled with by the National or General Government. This might have been true to a certain extent *before* the rebellion, but as these States have, *as States*, rebelled against that General Government, they have by that act forfeited all the rights they had (as States) previous to such act, just as an individual criminal forfeits his personal rights under the law by a violation of the law made for the protection of all. You may tell me that a general confiscation of the slaves would, notwithstanding my proposed ransom money, work injury to particular persons. Possibly; so does the punishment of the individual work the injury of disgrace to his family and friends. Yet our sympathy for such persons does not prevent us from meting out that justice required for the good of society.

The few persons who might possibly be inconvenienced by a general confiscation of slaves stand to the entire Union as does the innocent members of a convict's family to the community. The misfortunes of neither, growing out of consanguinity or accident of locality, should weigh naught against the interests of the great whole. We desire to end the rebellion. Will a general confiscation of slaves do this? Yes, for the reason given above. It will weaken the enemy. You say it is "vindictive." You do not say it is inefficacious—in fact you admit its efficacy in referring it to the President for use as a war power, to be used in his discretion. Will it not be as "vindictive" when used by him as "a war power," as if used by him as the Executive of a Congressional resolve or enactment? If it will be efficacious when used by the President, why not let Congress request or require him to use it? Why spend three millions a day in prolonging a war which, according to your own showing, can be speedily ended? You say it is "vindictive" to end the war by the means proposed. Our enemies shoot our pickets from ambuscades, and when we propose to weaken him by taking away his main source of strength, you tell us it is "vindictive." Our sons and brothers are killed by the poisoned meats and drugged drinks, yet when we propose a way to end the war, and bring them to their homes, you tell us it is "vindictive."

These rebels bury our dead martyrs with their faces downward, looking toward that region to which their murderers will go, and when we propose to remove the living companions of these murdered ones beyond the reach of their barbarism, by depriving them of their great strength, we are told that it is "vindictive."

The skulls of our brave boys are made into drinking cups by the very rebels whose slaves we propose to confiscate, and when we say deprive them of the power to polish more skulls, we are accused of being " vindictive."

Good men volunteering to uphold their country's flag, and pour out their blood like water in its defense, are Bull Run-ed and Ball's Bluff-ed to untimely graves, and when we suggest a mode of ending such wholesale murdering, we are called " vindictive."

Liberal citizens contribute freely to relieve the needs of families whose supporters are fighting our battles, and when we point a way to stop these drains on our charities, we are told we are " vindictive."

When loyal men from Rebel States, like Polk, Maynard, Brownlow, and others, whose homes have been desolated, and their wives and daughters foully abused, call on us to adopt this remedy *for their protection*, we are told we are " vindictive."

The slaves of these murdering rebels offer their services to our armies as guides, pilots and messengers, and when we propose to invite them to do more of this righteous work by an act of confiscation, we are met by the cry of vindictiveness. The only reliable information we have ever had of the rebels' condition has been furnished by the slaves of these rebels, and if we ask for more such help we are " vindictive."

Had our Generals been less vindictive in returning these loyal black men to their white rebel masters, and more energetic in using the information they brought them, we should to-day be much nearer the end of the rebellion than we are.

It seems to me, Mr. Editor, that you have used the wrong word—instead of vindictive say justice, and you will be right.

STATE RIGHTS.

(From the Continental Monthly, May, 1862.)

The theory of State Rights, as expounded by its advocates in its application to the several States of the American Union, is subversive of all government, and calculated to destroy our political organization. Its tendency is to weaken the central government by minute divisions of the power necessary for its maintenance. Without power to make its authority respected, no government can live. The doctrine of State Sovereignty detracts from this authority by lessening the power which upholds it. Thirty-four States, each claiming exclusive authority to act independently on any given subject, have only one thirty-fourth part of the strength that they would have, were they all acting under and controlled by one

3

central head. That central head in our Union is the Federal Government, formed by and growing out of the Constitution, and it must exist for the protection of each of its thirty-four members, as well as for itself, the connecting power. Its acts must not be disputed by any one of the States or by any number of them acting in concert. If one or more States may defy the central authority, or attempt to withdraw from its government, any other State may do likewise, to the ruin of the political fabric erected at so much cost, and in its place would spring up scores of weak and unprotected communities. But, says the State rights advocate, this central power will have too much authority, too much control over the States; will become despotic, and in time destroy the liberties of the people. How? By whom will those liberties be destroyed? This central power, styled the Federal Government, is formed by the people, is of the people, is for the people, and has only such power as the people gave it; and thus being of and from the people, it (or they) can not destroy its (or their) own liberties. Were our government hereditary instead of elective; were our institutions monarchical instead of republican: had we privileged classes perpetuated by primogeniture, there might be some danger of placing too much power in the hands of the Federal Government; but formed as our institutions are, framed as our Constitution is, educated as our people are, there can be no fear of having the central power or general Federal Government too strong, or its authority supreme. Without strength there can be no authority; without authority there can be no respect; without respect there can be no government; without government there can be no civilization. The doctrine of State rights, as applied to the communities forming the American Union, elevates the State over the nation, demands that the Federal shall yield to the State laws, and completely ignores the supremacy of the united authority of the whole people. This theory, carried out logically, would make counties equal to States; towns equal to counties; wards and districts equal to towns; neighborhoods equal to districts and wards; and to come down to the last application of the principal, every one man in a neighborhood equal to the whole, in fact, superior, if the State rights doctrine be true, that the State is supreme within its own limits. The application of this principle ends society by destroying the order based on authority, and placing the State above the Nation, and the individual above the State. Civilized societies are but the aggregation of persons coming or remaining together for mutual interest and protection. This mutual interest requires certain rules for the protection of the weak from the encroachments of the strong in the society, as well as from outside enemies. These rules take the form of laws. These laws must be administered; their administration requires power. This power is placed in the hands of certain members of this society, community, or State, as the case may be, for the good of the whole State, and each individual claiming protection from the State, or whose interest is promoted by being a member thereof, is under moral as well as legal obligations to submit to this authority thus exercised by the chosen executors of the public will. Rights that might pertain to one man on an island by himself, do not attach to man in civilized communities. There he must not go beyond the landmarks established by law, and he agrees to this arrangement by remaining in the State or community. The same principle is equally applicable to the States of the American Union. Before the adoption of the Federal Constitution they were separate, distinct, and so far as any central head or supreme governing power was concerned, independent States, or, in fact, sovereignties. True, they had tried to get along under a sort of confederation agreement, a kind of temporary alliance for offensive and defensive ends, but which failed from its own inherent weakness, from the lack of that cohesiveness which nothing but centralization can give. Prior to the adoption of the Federal Constitution, these different States were like so many different individuals outside of any regular society; were merely so many isolated aggregations of non-nationalized individuals. Experience showed them their unfortunate condition; as separate States they had no strength to repel a common enemy, no credit, no money, no authority, commanded no respect. So it is with an individual outside of society. These States were then in the enjoyment —no, not in the enjoyment, but merely in possession—of State rights to the fullest extent. They had the right to be poor ; the right to be weak ; the right to get in debt; the right to issue bills of credit, (was any one found who thought it right to take them?) the right to wage war with any of their neighbors; the right to do any and all acts pertaining to an independent sovereignty; but these rights were not all that the people of these States desired; and after trying the independent and the confederate State policy until experience had shown the utter fallacy of both, they met in convention and passed the present Constitution, and formed themselves into ONE NATION. This Constitution, compact, copartnership, confederation, combination, or whatever it may be called, was and is the written foundation (voluntarily made) on which the NATION is built and maintained.

The charter, instrument, or Constitution, defines, by common consent and mutual agreement of the parties voluntarily forming it, the powers, rights, and duties of the National Government growing out of and based on this Constitution. Among the powers thus delegated to the National or Federal Government, and to be used by the legislative authority thereof, are the following:

" Article I.—Section 8.

" The Congress shall have power—

" 1. To lay and collect taxes, duties, imposts, and excises, to pay the debts and provide for the common defense and general welfare of the United States ; but all duties, imposts, and excises shall be uniform throughout the United States.

" 2. To borrow money on the credit of the United States.

" 3. To regulate commerce with foreign nations, and among the several States, and with the Indian tribes.

" 4. To establish a uniform rule of naturalization, and uniform laws on the subject of bankruptcies, throughout the United States.

" 5. To coin money, regulate the value thereof, and of foreign coin, and fix the standard of weights and measures.

" 6. To provide for the punishment of counterfeiting the securities and current coin of the United States.

" 7. To establish post-offices and post-roads

" 8. To promote the progress of science and useful arts, by securing, for limited times, to authors and inventors the exclusive right to their respective writings and discoveries.

" 9. To constitute tribunals inferior to the Supreme Court.

" 10. To define and punish piracies and felonies committed on the high seas, and offenses against the law of nations.

" 11. To declare war, grant letters of marque and reprisal, and make rules concerning captures on land and water.

" 12. To raise and support armies ; but no appropriation of money to that use shall be for a longer term than two years.

" 13. To provide and maintain a navy.

" 14. To make rules for the government and regulation of the land and naval forces.

" 15. To provide for calling forth the militia to execute the laws of the Union, suppress insurrections, and repel invasions.

" 16. To provide for organizing, arming, and disciplining the militia, and for governing such part of them as may be employed in the service of the United States, reserving to the States respectively the appointment of the officers, and the authority of training the militia, according to the discipline prescribed by Congress.

" 18. To make all laws which shall be necessary and proper for carrying into execution the foregoing powers, and all other powers vested by this Constitution in the government of the United States, or in any department or officer thereof."

The first two words in this section—" the Congress "—completely annul the separate integrity of States. The Congress of what, and for what ? The Congress of the United States, acting for the United States, as a unit, a whole, a union. The only allusion in this section to anything like a right existing in any State after the adoption of the Constitution, is the right to officer the militia, and these officers are to 'train' the militia, *under the direction of Congress,* and not under State laws—a clause which of itself strikes a decisive blow at the theory of independent State rights. In no one of these specifications is there a single allusion to any " State." Every power enumerated is given to the " *United* States," to the " Union " formed by virtue of the Constitution. Never was there a more perfect absorption of atoms into one mass, than in these specifications; but to make the principle still stronger, and as if to remove any doubt as to " State rights," the first clause of the Ninth Section of the same Article prohibits any State from importing certain persons after a given date, which, when it arrived (in 1808), Congress passed a national law stopping the slave-trade—a trade that some of the States would have been glad to encourage, or, at least, allow, if they had had authority to do so. This right was taken from them by the Constitution, in the year 1808; up to that time they had that right; but after that date the right no longer existed, and Congress passed the law referred to, in accordance with the power given them by this clause of the Constitution.

But this First Article of Section Nine is not all in that section that smothers State rights; for Article Five declares that vessels bound to or from one State need not enter, clear, or pay duties in another. Why this specification, if the States were to be supreme in their own limits? (and this doctrine of State rights is, in its essence, supremacy.) Independent States exact clearances and entrances, and demand duties from foreign vessels, but never from their own. State rights are ignored in this Article. But to prevent any possibility of any State ever exercising the right of sovereignty now claimed by the advocates of this most pernicious doctrine, from which has grown the present gigantic rebellion, Section Ten, of the same Article, goes on to declare that—

" 1. No State shall enter into any treaty, alliance, or confederation; grant letters of marque and reprisal; coin money; emit bills of credit; make anything but gold and silver coin a tender in payment of debts; pass any bill of attainder, *ex post facto* law, or law impairing the obligation of contracts; or grant any title of nobility.

" 2. No State shall, without the consent of Congress, lay any imposts or duties on imports or exports, except what may be absolutely necessary for executing its inspection laws; and the net produce of all duties and imposts laid by any State on imports or exports, shall be for the use of the treasury of the United States; and all such laws shall be subject to the revision and control of the Congress. No State shall, without the consent of Congress, lay any duty on tonnage, keep troops or ships of war in

time of peace, enter into any agreement or compact with another State or
with a foreign power, or engage in war."

Language cannot be stronger; intentions were never more clearly expressed; thoughts were never more explicitly set forth in words. Nothing is left for doubt; all is concise, positive, and binding. Nothing is
left to be guessed at; nothing left that could be construed to mean that
States "may" or "may not." " SHALL " and " SHALL NOT," are the words
used to define what the States are to do or not to do. The very slight
"right" given to the States to lay duties for executing their inspection
laws, carries with it a proviso, or command, that the proceeds of such
duties must be paid into the National Treasury, and the very laws that
the States might pass for this purpose must be approved by " THE CON-
GRESS." What Congress? The Congress of the UNITED STATES—of the
UNION. Every vestige of State sovereignty, of " State rights," is utterly
annihilated in these clauses.

Independent sovereign States may, and do make treaties, alliances,
grant letters of marque, or coin money; in fact, no " State " or sovereignty
can exist without these powers; and the fact that these powers are all
taken from and denied to the States of the American Union, is conclusive
proof that the framers of the Constitution did not intend to allow the
States the sovereignty now claimed for them, and which the rebellious
States are endeavoring to maintain. This heresy must be exorcised now
and forever.

Is there any thing more in the Constitution (and bear in mind that no
right is claimed for any State except in accordance with this instrument,
which is still in full force except in those rebellious States where this disorganizing doctrine of " State rights " has uncontrolled sway) making the
Union supreme and the States subordinate? What says the following
section?

" Full faith and credit shall be given in each State to the public acts,
records, and judicial proceedings of every other State. And the Congress
may, by General laws, prescribe the manner in which such acts, records,
and proceedings shall be proved, and the effect thereof."

A State, therefore, *may* so legislate, that is, it *may* have acts and records, but each other State SHALL give to the records and proceedings of
all the rest "full faith and credit." Does not this enactment thoroughly
negative all theories of the exclusive supremacy of State rights? Independent sovereign States do not, in the absence of treaties, give any faith

or credit to the records or proceedings of other independent States. Our States are not only compelled to do this, by this section, but must do so in accordance with the manner prescribed by "the Congress" of the UNITED STATES, of the UNION, and of the NATION. No other Congress is mentioned.

"SECTION 2.

"The citizens of each State shall be entitled to all privileges and immunities of citizens in the several States."

By this clause a native or naturalized citizen of Maine can conduct business, hold and convey real estate (the highest civil, social, and judicial tests of citizenship) in the State of Georgia. The citizen of Minnesota can do likewise in New York and so of each and in all the States. Independent States or supreme sovereignties do not allow these privileges to any but their own citizens. The United States do not, neither do other nations. Citizenship must precede the right to hold and convey real estate. All governments are naturally jealous of the alien. By this clause, no American citizen can be an alien in any State of the American Union. He is a citizen of the nation. No State can pass any law demanding more of a citizen not born, though residing within its limits, than from one born therein, or place him under any restrictions not common to the native or other citizen of such State. Not a vestige of "State" exclusiveness is there in the clause. Every idea of State supremacy is blotted out by it. A heavier blow is, however, dealt at State rights in the following section:

"The United States shall guarantee to every State in this Union a republican form of government, and shall protect each of them against invasion, and, on application of the Legislature, or of the Executive (when the Legislature can not be convened), against domestic violence."

The greatest of all rights that an independent State can or may have is the right to adopt its own form of government; but this clause completely destroys such right on the part of any State of this Union to frame its own form of government. No State, for example, can have a monarchical government; since the United States are to guarantee a *republican* form: and no State can adopt an hereditary or theocratic government, because the UNITED STATES are bound to give each State a republican government. In like manner we might run through all the forms of government that have ever blessed or cursed our race, without finding one which can be adopted by any State of this Union, except the single form of "republican," named in the Constitution. But can a State, bereft of the right to frame its own mode of government, be said to be possessed of "*sovereign* State rights," or could a more effectual provision against their development have been formed than this?

"This Constitution, and the laws of the United States which shall be made in pursuance thereof, and all treaties made, or which shall be made, under the authority of the United States, shall be the supreme law of the land; and the Judges in every State shall be bound thereby; anything in the Constitution or laws of any State to the contrary notwithstanding.

"The Senators and Representatives before-mentioned, and the members of the several STATE LEGISLATURES, and all executive and judicial officers, both of the United States and of the SEVERAL STATES, shall be bound by oath or affirmation to support this Constitution."

This Constitution, these laws, these treaties, *shall be the supreme law*, no matter what "State" constitutions and "State" laws may declare. "Shall!" is the word, and there can be no doubt as to its meaning. Again, members of the State Legislatures, and all officers of the several States, "shall" be bound to support the "Constitution." Where are the "State rights" in these clauses? Every State and every State official is made subordinate to and an executive of the acts of the "United States," and the United States constitutes a "*nation.*" This is the only word which meets our case. WE ARE A NATION, not a "tenant-at-will sort of confederacy."

The waters of the Bay of New York and the Hudson river flow entirely within the States of New York and New Jersey. One of the vested rights of an independent State, is that known as "eminent domain," or supreme ownership, implying control. Apply this doctrine of State rights in this case, or rather, allow it to be applied by the States named above, and they could prevent the navigation of these waters by any but their own citizens or those to whom they might grant that privilege. If this doctrine of State rights is sound, these two States would have the right to levy tolls or duties on every vessel that sails those waters, as the State of New York exacts tolls on her canals. Such power thus exercised, would cripple commerce, inconvenience the public, and utterly destroy all comity between the States. This exacting tolls for navigation of waters is one of the most offensive systems left us by past generations. It is so odious that modern governments decline to submit to it in cases where there is no doubt as to "State rights," as in that of the "Sound Dues" exacted by Denmark. If, however, the State is supreme within its limits, it has a perfect right to exacts such tolls. But no State in this nation has any such right under the Constitution. Its existence would destroy the Union by placing each State under the laws and exactions of either one of the others. The troubles growing out of such exactions would beget dispute; these disputes would beget open strife, which would end in open rupture and the downfall of the NATIONAL UNION.

The "UNITED STATES," the "Union," the "Nation," are *supreme.* The States, *as States,* are subordinate; as "parts," they are inferior to the "whole." The "State rights" doctrine is wrong, disorganizing, destructive of national life, and must be destroyed.

Again, one grand evidence of a nation's or a people's civilization, is found in the correspondence, written and printed, conducted by the citizens. Barbarians have and need no correspondence. Civilization needs it, and can not exist without it. A migratory people like ours have more correspondence than older and less migratory nations. A citizen emigrating from Vermont to Illinois must correspond with the friends of his old home. The old friend in Vermont must know how the absent one " gets along in the world." To conduct this correspondence, the postal or mail service was devised. Before its existence the communication between separated friends and business people was uncertain, irregular, and mere matter of chance, to be conveyed by stray travelers, or not interchanged at all. The *necessities* of civilization brought the postal or mail service into action. To conduct this service over a nation, requires the right of passage through the entire limits of the nation. This right, to be available, must have power to enforce its own requirements. It must be *central,* CONTROLING, SUPREME. Without these, there would be no safety, no system, no uniformity, no regularity. To insure these to all the people of the States, the Constitution has wisely placed these powers in " THE CONGRESS" of the Union, of the "NATION." In accordance with the powers thus vested in Congress, our present postal or mail service has been created. No State has a right to interfere with the transportation of the national mails. "The UNITED STATES MAIL," is the term used. If any State had a right to establish a mail within its own limits, it would also have the right to prohibit or curtail the transportation of other States' mail through its limits. This right would destroy the entire system, and break up the interchange of correspondence so essential to our civilization. If the States had any such right, they could affix discriminating tariffs on the correspondence of other States passing through them. The State of New York, could, if this right existed, make the letters sent over its roads by the people of Massachusetts to the people of Ohio, pay just such tariffs for the "right of passage" as it might choose. The absurdity and utter unreasonableness of this claimed right is so apparent as to need no argument against it.

The exercise of this pretended right by the Southern States has caused the present rebellion. But for this doctrine we should not be expending over a million a day in supporting six hundred thousand men in camp, who ought to be producers of life instead of missionaries of death. This war is the legitimate result of this heresy of "State rights." If this doctrine had never been put in practice, we should not now have slavery to curse us with its degrading, inhumanizing influences. Slavery exists in *violation* of the Constitution. Slavery was never established by that document. The States violated it in their attempts at legalizing it. All their laws declaring that the *status* of the child must be that of the mother, are but so many " BILLS OF ATTAINDER," working " CORRUPTION OF BLOOD;" and every State, as well as Congress itself, was, and is positively prohibited by the Constitution from passing any such bill or law; and should we ever succeed in having any but a pro-slavery, slave-catching Supreme Court, all these laws will be annulled by their own unconstitutionality. True, there were slaves at the time the Constitution was adopted, but all then living are now dead; and but for this doctrine of " State rights," there never would have been any State law making the child of a slave mother also a slave; but for this doctrine, no such bill of attainder would have been passed, or if passed, it never could have been enforced; and we should not to-day be listening to the cries of four millions of slaves, nor have the homes of thousands of honest citizens made desolate by the absence of loved ones. But for this terrible doctrine, " the click of hammers closing rivets up," would not now be giving " dreadful note of preparation." But for this heresy, subversive of all law, of all order, of all nationality, we should not to-day be at war for our existence. But for this doctrine, and the right claimed by some of the States to extend their " bills of attainder," working corruption of blood over the entire Union, we should not have our homes filled with grief and our streets covered with the funeral pageants of brave men killed in defense of the Union. We want no more evidence of the accursed doctrine of " State rights." We are a UNION—a NATION. We must have NATIONAL LAWS, NATIONAL INSTITUTIONS, NATIONAL FREEDOM. We have had too much of State law, too much of State rights, too much of State slavery. The NATION MUST BE SUPREME. The States must be subordinate. As we uphold and perpetuate the national authority, so will be our existence as a people. As we detract from this, so will be our weakness and downfall.

GOD PRESERVE THE NATION!

REPUBLICAN CENTRAL COMMITTEE.

THE following preamble and resolutions, introduced by Mr. Tousey, were unanimously passed by the Republican Central Committee, at its regular meeting, on Wednesday evening, July 9:

Whereas, The condition of our country renders it the duty of all good men to stand by the Government in its efforts to crush rebellion; therefore, be it

Resolved, That this Central Committee of the Republican party of the city and county of New York, as a whole, and each member thereof for himself individually, pledges the Committee to aid the Administration in its efforts to suppress the rebellion; and be it further

Resolved, That this Committee views with utter abhorrence the attempt of *Northern traitors* to aid the rebels by efforts to divide the people of the loyal States, and that any party, or any man, who attempts, in these perilous times, to attract attention from, and divide the odium justly fixed on, rebels in arms, is as much a traitor to the Union as those in arms for its destruction.

Resolved, That the Government ought, in this hour of necessity, to avail itself of all the means within its reach, inviting and accepting the aid of every person willing and able to serve his country.

New York Tribune, July 10, 1862.

THE STANTON ORDER.

WE publish the following from an esteemed citizen, with the simple remark, that he has misconceived the tenor and spirit of the article to which he refers. We offer no objection to the adoption of adequate measures to prevent "skedaddlers" from their duty from escaping the necessary burdens of war; but do object to the promulgation of an order which, in its sweeping terms and stringency, will leave the false impression on the mind of every foreigner that the people of the United States generally are cowards or traitors. This inevitable inference will give "aid and comfort" to our revilers abroad and to our foes in the South, who will naturally conclude that the indifference or hostility of the people of the North to the war is so deep and wide-spread as to require the most stringent and sweeping measures of the Government to keep them up to their duty. The rebels will take comfort accordingly, just as we did when we found that they were obliged to impress their soldiers:

" *Editor Frank Leslie's Illustrated Newspaper :*

" I protest against the spirit of your leader in your issue of last week. That article is calculated to give 'aid and comfort' to the enemies of the Government at home and among the rebels. The order of the Secretary of War, which you denounce so strongly, manifests more of a spirit of determination in the right direction than anything that has been done in Washington for a year. We are blockading the enemy's coasts. For what ? To keep out such things as they need : as munitions of war, men, and *information.* The great complaint among loyal men has been, that the Government has been too lax in its efforts to restrain information from reaching the rebels. The present order of non-intercourse will help to keep back this information, as well as to prevent men from escaping from military duty ; in fact, it will act as an 'internal land blockade.' Heretofore the sympathizers with the rebels could go and come as they chose ; now they can not, and thus a great good will be accomplished. No truly loyal man, desiring to aid the Government and do his duty, will be prevented from going and coming as his business may require. This order will affect none but those whose existence and actions demanded its enforcement. I am glad it has been issued. Suppose you are put to the trouble of getting a passport ? If the system will produce the result intended, you and all other good citizens can well afford to help it on. I am glad that order was issued. I am also pleased with the other order preventing secession-advocating, rebel-sympathizing, enlistment-retarding brawlers from spouting their treasonable doctrines in the Loyal States. Don't find any more fault with such orders."—*Leslie's Illustrated Paper*, August 30, 1862.

AN EARNEST VOICE.

(*From the Boston Banner of Light.*)

THERE are comparatively few men engaged in commercial pursuits, and daily occupied by the cares of business, who have much to do with the commerce of ideas, or can find leisure for a critical observation of " the signs of the times." There are, however, occasional exceptions, and Mr. Sinclair Tousey (firm of Ross & Tousey, the great news agents of New York) is conspicuous among them. Notwithstanding the protracted indisposition of his partner —which has long rendered him incapable of giving his personal attention to business—Mr. Tousey finds time to observe the progress of events, and to write occasionally for the daily press and the magazines. Some time since, he contributed a paper to the *Knickerbocker,* on " Emancipation," which stirred the slow blood of its conservative readers, and excited some discussion in the papers. Mr. Tousey is a gentleman of great frankness, and, when he has any thing to say, is accustomed to speak out loud, without the slightest regard to latitudinal considerations, or the velvet-slippered servants of the Van Winkle family. We are bound to respect every man who respects the rights and interests of all men. Mr. Tousey appears to be such a man who dares to strike at Wrong, whether it be concealed beneath the mitre or behind a throne.

From a late issue of the New York *Daily Times*, we extract the following earnest and unstudied exhortation to the freemen of the North:

NORTHMEN, TAKE COURAGE.

The world moves. The Star of Freedom is rising higher and higher, to be eclipsed only by the more glorious rays of the Sun of Universal Liberty, whose bright light will soon illuminate our whole political hemisphere. The civilization of Freedom is crushing out the great barbarism of Slavery. The moral atmosphere is being purified by the storms of agitation. As tides keep oceans pure, so do great thoughts and just principles purify the political and social pools of human stagnation, human wrongs. From the far-off shores of the Pacific (significant of peace) come great tornadoes of pure air. From the North, land of snow and ice (emblematic of purity and strength), come great torrents of clear waters. These western winds and northern waters are sweeping down toward the Gulf, in one grand, sublime current of onward power for good, for Freedom, for civilization.

NORTHMEN, BE HOPEFUL. With your hopes blend watchfulness. Truer to-day than ever before is it that "*eternal vigilance is the price of liberty.*" The homes of Freedom must be guarded by the "watch-fires that never go out." The West, North and Northwest winds and waters have carried traitorous Senators from the "inner chamber," have borne lukewarm, rebel-sympathizing Generals from command; have swept imperious, spying correspondents into prison; have carried contumacious witnesses into congressional lock-ups. Northmen! see that these movements go on. Put the broad shoulders of honest workers to the car-wheels now rolling on to Freedom. Let the hard hands that "break" the strong greenswards of the Western prairies grow harder in "breaking" the yoke of the bondman. Let the East men and the West men and the North men join hand in hand in rolling on the chariot-wheels of American liberty, till our Flag shall in truth wave over "the land of the free," undimmed by the presence of a single slave. Northmen! be workers, be agitators; be to the moral atmosphere what the winds are to the natural. Let your commotions purify. Discuss, educate, enlighten. Be missionaries of liberty; be apostles of freedom ; be the flag-bearers of civilization. Encourage your Congressional representatives in their deeds for freedom; censure them if they falter. Be bold for the right; be cowardly only in wrong. Be strong for justice; be weak only when unjust. Demand justice for all; allow injustice to none. Let your motto be "one freedom, one country, one flag, one people," knowing no distinction but that of merit. Be thankful for the past, trustful of the present, hope and watch for the future ; and as you act in this great crisis, so will be your lot in the time that is coming.

[The above was published about the time that Mr. Bright, a Senator in Congress from the State of Indiana, was expelled from the Senate for sympathy with the great Southern Rebellion of 1861. About the same time two or three very prominent correspondents of the New York Herald were locked up for prying into government secrets and having too much sympathy with the rebels. It is to these that allusions are made in the above article.] *Winter of* 1861—62

(*From the New York Ledger*, May 24, 1862.)

GALLOWS CANDIDATES.

To the Editor of the New York Ledger :

Loyal men believe that the leaders of the present diabólical rebellion should be hanged. Justice will be satisfied with nothing less, nay, she demands more. Justice, in the old mythology, is represented with bandaged eyes. The Justice of our day has her eyes *uncovered*. She sees that the foes of the Union are not all in the ranks of the rebels. She finds our worst enemies in our own camps, in our own high places, and she demands their lives as a partial expiation of the outrageous wickedness perpetrated by the worst scoundrels that ever cursed a country or disgraced humanity. She demands that those wingless human vampyres called "CONTRACTORS," who are fattening on a nation's blood, and rioting in the wealth wrung from the very vitals of an afflicted people, should be hanged on a gallows higher that any ever dreamed of by ancient or modern Hamans. Justice demands this at the hands of her officers, and the honest public second the demand.

The preservation of the Union required men. Mothers sent forth their sons to "do and die" in its defense; wives sent their husbands, sisters their brothers ; fathers marched side by side with their "only sons," all animated by the purest motives that ever prompted a human deed. The country poured forth its treasures as freely as the torrents that flow down its mighty streams in spring time. But with and about these glorious sacrifices, these magnificent treasures, lurked a thousand ghouls, a thousand were-wolves ready to pounce on and suck dry the blood of our brave men, and greedily plunder the National Treasury. Men volunteering to fight the battles of the country have been barbarously killed piecemeal by the poisonous food supplied by rapacious contractors. Good men, used to home comforts, ready to lay down their lives in battle, have been maimed by frost, bitten by the cold—aye, *frozen*—actually frozen from lack of the decent clothing for which the Government had paid these Robber Contractors. Are they not "Gallows Candidates?" It makes the brain reel and the nerves tremble, to reflect on these most infernal wrongs, wreaked on our brave men by such Ishmaelites. *Let them be hanged.* Some of those men have by a "commission on purchases" for the Government, made as much money in one day as paid to a whole regiment of honest men in the ranks, the meanest one of whom is a king to the best of these plundering "brothers-in-law contractors." Congress fixes the pay of the soldier, why not of the contractor? *The soldier fights for the country.* The contractor robs for *himself*. *Let him be hanged.* Congress is about to lay a heavy tax on the people. The people are willing to be taxed, but they are not willing to be robbed by swindling contractors, and taxed to pay the robbers. Let Congress lay a heavy hand, yes, a heavy "fist" on the throats of these money-getting rascals. *Let them be hanged*, no matter if they be "brothers-in-law" of cabinet officers. The higher the position of the offender, the higher ought his gallows to be, and the more prompt his punishment.

THE NEW YORK TIMES ON GOVERNOR ANDREW.

To the Editor of the New York Tribune :

Sir—*The N. Y. Times* pretends to be a loyal paper, yet in its issue of the 14th it manifests the same spirit that conducts the *concession* and other rebel-sympathizing sheets. It inserts Governor Andrew's order for enrolling the fighting men of his State, and gives that order with an editorial notice that must delight the souls (if they have any), of all King Jeff's subjects.

The Times hates Governor Andrew, and all who, like him, believe in human freedom. It pretends to the contrary; but the most of its articles, that lean either way, lean toward slavery, or toward that line of policy that conserves the "institution." Governor Andrew is a representative man. He is the head of a representative State. His people and himself are full of positive loyalty—not that sort of loyalty that fills the columns of *The Times*, and which is any thing by turns and nothing long, except in the length of its "trimming" propensities.

If there is one Governor of the loyal States whom the rebels and their Northern sympathizers would like to hang first, that Governor is he of Massachusetts, and *The Times*, true to its instincts of hate to the negro, is encouraging that spirit. It ill becomes any loyal press to try to make Massachusetts or her Governor odious to the people of other States. Her record in this rebellion is too pure; her citizens too patriotic; her Governor too energetic for the right.

The Times will fail to set the Federal Government against the old Commonwealth. It says: "the question of employing blacks in a military capacity is one for the National Government to decide." It forgets (intentionally?) that the Government only represents the people in this, as in all other matters, and when they demand that the blacks shall help to maintain the Government that protects them in person and property, it (the Government) will enforce that demand, and surely there can be no better way to learn the people's wants than by their Governors' action, especially when the people respond to their Governors as they do in Massachusetts.

The Times had no censure for Governor Sprague for the same act (in spirit). Why? Governor S—— is not identified with the anti-slavery idea of the North. Governor A—— is. That is enough to arouse the ire of that paper. It will not do, *Mr. Times*. The great ball is rolling on, and if you do not get out of its way it will roll over you and all like you.—*N. Y. Tribune*, August 16, 1862.

NORTHERN TRAITORS.

To the Editor of The New York Tribune:

Sir—Armed rebellion at the South receives the armed attention of the Government. Unarmed treason at the North should receive the unarmed but none the less summary attention of that same Government. We are in a great rebellion. The existence of your national Government is in imminent danger. Treason has armed hundreds of thousands for its destruction. These armed traitors are all in one section of our country. Another section is in arms for its defense. In this latter section there are hundreds, perhaps thousands, whose political antecedents and desire for the trade of the rebellious section brought them to sympathize with that section, not daring to subject themselves to the penalties of offended law, or to the bitter contempt of their fellow-citizens, by open and avowed acts against their Governments, yet being determined to do all they can with personal safety, coward-like, and with diabolical malice, resort to the apparently more safe and just as efficacious mode of aiding the rebellion, by attempts at dividing the North against itself; and hence the traitorous cry of "Hang abolitionists and secessionists together." The odium that should centre on and burn deep into the hearts of armed rebels, these peace-preaching Judases try to divide, and place on a great portion of law-abiding, Government-upholding citizens, by demagogue howls and grog-shop-party-catch-words, that appeal to the baser passions and lower prejudices of the lowest of the discontented scum that curses society with its presence. These ever-galvanized corpses of a once great political organization know, from past experience, the power of union and the weakness of disunion, and, fearing that the unity of the North will speedily and thoroughly crush the most infernal rebellion that ever outraged a nation or disgraced mankind, coolly and deliberately set about dividing the low people of the North by any and every means within their reach. To divide the North is to weaken the North. To weaken the North is to strengthen the rebellious South. These northern traitors desire to aid the rebellion, and hence their effort to create dissension among us of the loyal North. Any party, or any man, be he a city mayor out of office or a renegade editor in full feather, that attempts, by word or deed, to render any part of the people of the loyal North odious to any other part of that people, is a traitor at heart, and the love of his country is not in him or in that party. Loyal men should shun all such as moral lepers, whose touch brings death, and whose very breath breeds pestilence. Governments should mark them. State and civil authorities should proscribe them. Officers of the law should convict them. Courts should punish them as promoters of disorder. Whosoever is not for the Government is against it. These traitorous dissensionists of the North are not for the Government. They had rather see the Union destroyed than to see it saved, if its salvation caused them the loss of party influence. With these men, party is all ; union, government, country, are naught. Hence their attacks on the *personnel* of the administration. They intend to make the present government of the people odious in the sight of the people, thus weaken it, thus cripple its powers, thus help

4

the rebellion, hoping, in the confusion of divisions thus created among us, to ride into power, and then hastily patch up a speedy and dishonorable peace, at the cost of the loyal States and to the disgrace of the nation.

Peace-preaching, dissension-creating treason is as dangerous as treason in arms. Beware of it ! Strangle it ! Treason in this form attacks cabinet ministers while lauding the President. Why ? It desires to weaken the Government, and not daring to openly attack the people's chosen head, it covertly stabs the President through the bodies of his recognized advisers. This kind of treason hopes and aims to tie the hands of the Government by false accusations and intolerable abuse of particular members of the National Administration ; thus weaken it, and by this hoped-for weakness, aid the rebels. No good citizen will depreciate the efforts of the Government, nor of its authorized officials, in this trying time. When men are talked of for position, it is proper to discuss their merits. While a proposed measure is not yet decided on, discussion is proper, but when men are in place and do their best, and when a plan has been decided on, let discussion end and action begin. The unity of the people of the loyal States is their salvation. Their diversion is their death.

New York, July 12, 1862.

JUDGE DALY AT THE NEW-ENGLAND DINNER.

To the Editor of The New York Tribune :

SIR—Foreigners have said that the American Judiciary does not command the respect due to the bench. That it is so is not surprising, when it is remembered how little some of our Judges respect themselves or others.

I am led to this thought by reading your report of Judge Daly's speech at the New England dinner. Here is a learned Judge, representing a society whose existence is fostered by our institutions—a Judge representing a people whom our laws have made, civilly and politically, equal to any of our citizens—here is this Judge, at a public dinner, at a time when the country that shelters his people is bleeding at every pore, when death stalks abroad at noon-day and rests not at night, when every household is draped in mourning, and grief sits in the market-place—here is this Judge, at such a time and under such circumstances, facetiously comparing our bone-covered battle-fields to a sportsman's cock-pit, and the legitimate Government of the Union to a "*game-cock*" fighting out of pure obstinacy! Not a word of condemnation for the rebels, who are murdering our sons and widowing our daughters—not a word of rebuke to their aiders and abettors at home and abroad—not a word of encouragement for those who are laying down their lives and expending their fortunes for the maintenance of that flag under whose folds this Judge's countrymen find asylum—not one word for the integrity of the Union—not one word for the supremacy of law over insurrection—not one word to show that he considers the rebels less justifiable in their work of death than the Government of the Union in its work of preserving the life of the nation; but, on the contrary, every word he utters, every idea he advances, serves to place the rebels on a par with the National Government. He jocosely styles both "game-cocks." A calm observer would say that the Judge had as much sympathy for one side as the other; in fact, one might almost say that he was "*a little more so*" for the ONE side, and that side NOT of the Union. Is it surprising that the American Judiciary is not respected? Other speeches of this Judge, on other occasions during the rebellion, have shown the same drift, and have passed unnoticed! I think it time to rebuke him.—*N. Y. Tribune*, Dec. 24, 1862.

DEMOCRATIC HOWLINGS.

Everybody not stone blind knows that there is a fixed determination on the part of the leaders of the democratic party to break down the administration and if possible thwart it in its efforts to crush the rebellion. The late charge of Recorder Hoffman is a part of the plan, which, if successfully inaugurated in this city, is to be universally adopted throughout the North. The democratic party is not yet ready to assume a position of forcible or armed opposition to the Federal Government (though it is surely drifting that way), but being bent on destroying the present constitutional authorities, that party is endeavoring by its partisan judges, by its traitorous orators, by its lying presses, to make the national administration odious with the people, and thus influence them to withhold men and money for the prosecution of the war for the Union. Is the disloyalty of the democratic party questioned? That party has learned from the ballot-box during the past ten years that the anti-slavery sentiment of the free States is growing much faster than the pro-slavery sentiment of those States, and that without the votes of their slave-breeding, women-whipping, baby-selling democratic compeers in the now rebellious States, they, the northern democrats, can never again hope to get control of the National Government. Hence their attempts to destroy the present administration by their howlings about " illegal arrests," " violation of personal rights," the " guarantees of the constitution," the " sacredness of the citizen," and so on, ad nauseaum. The democratic leaders, who drive the party in the North as their southern colleagues drive their slaves, knowing that our people are jealous of their rights, think and intend by these howlings to arouse indignation against the Government, and thus destroy its power, and compel it to end the war on such terms as will suit the democratic rebels of the South—when these northern leaders of the once more united national democracy hope to reinstate themselves in Union offices, and again bow the nation down to that political god of modern democracy, negro slavery. This is the programme, and Recorder Hoffman and all other partisan judges like him and Judge Daly, are but doing the dirty work of secession in making grand jury charges and dinner speeches that serve to render the Government unpopular.—*Tribune*, December, 1862.

A JUST REBUKE.

(*From the New York Tribune*)

A number of men, of whom the public generally seem to know very little, are now going the rounds of the city and seeking to depreciate United States Treasury notes (greenbacks) by the purchase at a premium of two and one-half to three per cent. of our city bank bills. Who those persons are, or where they came from, or with whom they are directly connected—whether with northern banks or northern secessionists—nobody in particular seems to know, but there is no disputing the fact that they are so engaged in attempting to destroy public confidence in the Government. A case of the kind came to our knowledge yesterday. A well-dressed man, who for years has followed the business of buying up and furnishing small change to numerous store-keepers about the city, entered the store of Messrs. Ross & Tousey, and offered to purchase all the city bank-notes they had at two and one-half per cent. premium. Mr. Tousey, who was sitting in his office, attracted by the man's conversation with the clerk, came out and inquired his business, whereupon the person repeated his proposition to buy up all the city bank-notes they had in the store. Upon being asked the object, he commenced abusing the administration, characterizing it as a rotten abolition concern, and sought by every means in his power to depreciate the Government notes, pronouncing them as next to worthless. Mr. Tousey interrupted him in the midst of his tirade of abuse of the Government, telling him plainly that he was a true republican, and that he believed it the duty of every man to earnestly support the administration, no matter what might be his politics. He wanted no secessionists or secession sympathizers in his store, and concluded by informing the man that he would give him just one minute to leave the place ; and that if he didn't go by that time he would put him out. Furthermore, he never wanted him to show his face in the store again, on any pretext whatever. Secesh, deeming discretion the better part of valor, hurried out into the street.

RAILROADS AND BLACKS.

To the Editor of The New York Tribune :

Sir—I must fully indorse all you have said about the mean development of oppression just adopted by the Eighth Avenue Railroad. I will aid you in invoking legislative aid to correct that outrageous abuse just placed on colored people by that soulless company. Go ahead in that good work. I am credibly informed that the Superintendent, Col. May, *is an officer of the regular United States Army, now on quite a lengthy furlough*, drawing pay from the Government for services not rendered, and is now violating the *spirit* if not the letter of the orders of the War Office concerning colored persons. It is shameful that in these times any company should yield to the demands of the mob in the manner that this company has in this case. It is perfectly outrageous to see these poor people compelled to swelter along in the hot sun of a Sunday on their way to church, while drunken whites are allowed to crowd decent people entirely out of the cars. I refused to ride in the cars of the Sixth Avenue Company for years, on account of their colored peoples' cars, and now I shall apply the same to the Eighth avenue. I trust you will continue to show up the complete meanness of these companies.—*N. Y. Tribune*, Aug. 7, 1863.

Extract from the proceedings of the National Council of the U. L. A., held at Baltimore in June, 1864 :

WEDNESDAY, JUNE 8, 1864.

Council met at 3, and adjourned to 5 o'clock, P. M.
Council met at 5 o'clock, P. M.

Mr. Tousey, of New York, offered the following resolutions, which were unanimously adopted, viz. :

Resolved, That this National Council of the Union League of America, hereby most heartily approves and endorses the nominations made by the Union National Convention at Baltimore, on the 8th of June, 1864, of Abraham Lincoln for President, and of Andrew Johnson for Vice-President of the United States, and as we are bound by our obligation to do all in our power to elect true and reliable Union men, to all offices, and as the nominees of said Convention are the only candidates that can hope to be elected as loyal men, we regard it as the imperative duty of the members of the Union League to do all that lies in their power to secure their election.

Resolved, That this Council also earnestly approve and indorses the platform of principles adopted by said Convention.

Resolved, That we will, as individuals and as members of the Union League, do all in our power to elect said candidates.

On motion of Mr. Tousey, the injunction of secrecy was removed from these resolutions, and the Secretary directed to furnish a copy to the Associated Press.

UNION CENTRAL COMMITTEE.

The regular meeting of this body was held at their headquarters, corner Broadway and Twenty-third street, last evening, a large delegation being present. The following preamble and resolutions, introduced by Mr. Tousey, in regard to Messrs. Davis and Wade, were unanimously adopted:

Whereas, We are on the eve of a most important Presidential election, the result of which must gravely influence the destinies of the republic, thus rendering it necessary that the entire strength of the Union party should be brought to bear against the enemies of the country, whether such enemies are in arms in the field, or unarmed at home ; and

Whereas, There is danger of our strength being divided and frittered away by differences of opinion, not on vital points, as to men and measures, which divisions and differences must inure to the advantage of our political opponents (who are the enemies of the Government); and

Whereas, There has recently appeared in the public papers a manifesto over the names of Messrs. Wade and Davis, members of Congress, the tendency of which is to bring our Chief Magistrate into disrepute by weakening the confidence of the people in his administration of public

affairs, and thereby jeopardizing his re-election to the office for which he
has been nominated ; therefore be it

Resolved, By this Union Central Committee of the city and county of
New York, that we earnestly deprecate the publication of said manifesto,
and condemn the spirit which seems to have prompted its preparation and
publication.

Resolved, That we also condemn the practice of those pretended Union
men, who use their official, social, and party position to bring into disrepute the regularly nominated candidate of the party.

Resolved, That our faith in the judgment and patriotism of the President of the United States is unshaken, and we hereby renew our pledge
to do all in our power to insure his re-election.

Resolved, That copies of these resolutions, properly attested by the
officers of the Committee, be transmitted to the President and to Messrs.
Wade and Davis.

Tribune, Aug. 25, 1864.

GENERAL BUTLER'S PAPER TAX.

New York, April 8, 1864.

Major-General B. F. Butler :

Sir.—We have been informed that the privilege of selling newspapers
and other serial reading in the department under your command is
farmed out to one party, and that other dealers are not allowed " free
trade " in consequence of said regulation. Will you do us the favor to
inform us if this monopolizing regulation is in pursuance of your order,
for we are loth to believe that a Massachusetts man, fresh from the land
where the Press has, as it were, unrestricted circulation, could place any
obstruction in the way of a universal spread of intelligence among the
people. A reply will much oblige,

Yours, respectfully,

THE AMERICAN NEWS COMPANY.

SINCLAIR TOUSEY, *President*.

HEADQUARTERS EIGHTEENTH ARMY CORPS,
DEPARTMENT OF VIRGINIA AND NORTH CAROLINA,
FORTRESS MONROE, April 11, 1864.

Sir.—Your note of the 8th of April is received. You have not been
correctly informed. The privilege of selling daily and weekly newspapers, not published in my department, has been put exclusively in the
hands of one man, Mr. Bond, who pays the United States a certain tax
for the privilege, and he is held responsible for the loyal character of the

reading furnished the soldiers. By that means I have no difficulty in controlling the circulation of such papers as *The News*, *The World*, *The Catholic Repository*, *Boston Courier*, and other treasonable sheets of a like character. Every one agrees that there ought to be regulations to regulate the sale of poisonous liquors and drugs, which kill the body. How much more ought there to be a regulation of the sale of poisonous and pernicious writings that kill the soul. Mr. Bond pays a portion of the profits to the Government of the United States, and keeps the prices within proper limit. All other periodicals, such as magazines and pamphlets, are sold freely through the Department. If you have any complaints to make of his refusing to deal justly and properly for loyal newspapers, I should be happy to receive them and redress them.

I have the honor to be,

Very respectfully,

Your obedient servant,

BENJ. F. BUTLER,

Major-Gen. Commanding.

To S. TOUSEY, President American News Co.,

121 Nassau street, New York.

OFFICE OF THE AMERICAN NEWS COMPANY,

121 Nassau Street.

NEW-YORK, April 13, 1865.

Major-General B. F. BUTLER :

SIR—We beg leave to acknowledge the receipt of your favor of the 11th.

Admitting your power to inforce any regulation in your department, that your views of the public interest may dictate, we yet demur to the reason assigned for the regulation referred to, as we can not see how the levying of a tax on certain commodities, gives you any more control over the sale and distribution of such articles, than you possessed before the tax was levied—as the power to lay and collect taxes, carries with it the power to prohibit; in fact you say as much, when you declare that this regulation enables you to exclude certain disloyal sheets.

This mode of restricting the circulation of disloyal papers, cripples the sale of the loyal ones, by enhancing the cost thereof to the consumer, who pays the tax.

You understand this fact in political economy as well as any man in America.

You state that Mr. Bond, in addition to the tax he pays for farm privilege, also pays a share of the profits to the United States.

This, in our opinion, only adds so much more to the cost of the article to the consumer, and therefore, correspondingly restricts the circulation of the very papers that ought to go entirely uncrippled. We refer to those of loyal character. One instance will suffice to illustrate our point, if we are correctly informed. Before this tax was levied, the New York Ledger sold in your department for five or six cents; now *ten cents* are demanded for it.

This license does not come out of the pockets of the farmer, Mr. Bond; neither does the share of the profits allotted to the United States.

By the way, General, don't you think that the loyal, moneyed, and producing classes of our people can support the Government, without "taxing" the poor soldier for his newspaper? We incline to that opinion.

You say that there is no license needed to sell magazines and pamphlets; that they "are sold freely through the department." Will you allow us to state, General, that there is as rank treason published in magazines and pamphlets, as in newspapers; and being in more preservable form, has more lasting effect. Such magazines as the *Old Guard*, by C. C. Burr, and the thousands of disloyal, treasonable pamphlets, issued by the copper-heads of this and other cities, works more deadly harm to the soldiers, than many of the semi-secession papers.

Your tax system, you say, does not stop these from circulation in your department; but it does restrict the circulation of those of admitted loyalty. In regard to this particular class of reading matter (that is magazines and pamphlets), there seems to be a misunderstanding between yourself and the custom-house, here; for on applying to the Collector, last week, for permission to send reading matter, we were refused a permit, on the ground, that permits must issue from your department; and in consequence of such ruling here, we lost the sale of a large amount. We ask for correct information on this point, as we have frequent orders from your department for reading matter, other than newspapers. We also ask that this license system on the sale of daily and weekly newspapers be abrogated; that the division of the profits with the government be abolished, and there be adopted in place of both, an unrestricted system of free trade in all reading matter, that is allowed a sale at all in your department: believing that this course will best conduce to the interest of all concerned—producers, consumers, and the government too.

We do not ask for the circulation of any such works as you may deem improper; but we do ask that all such as you approve of, be left untrammeled with taxes and licenses.

Very respectfully, yours, &c.,

THE AMERICAN NEWS COMPANY.

SINCLAIR TOUSEY, *President.*

P. S.—We inclose a complaint from an old customer, at Portsmouth, to which we beg leave to call your attention.

HEADQUARTERS EIGHTEENTH ARMY CORPS,
DEPARTMENT OF VIRGINIA AND NORTH CAROLINA,

FORTRESS MONROE, April 17, 1864.

SIR—Mr. Bohn's privilege for selling newspapers was given him as the highest bidder, but with restriction that he should not raise the price of his periodicals, and he has not done so. You was misinformed upon that point. I have no doubt of the proposition of political economy that the tax upon an article is paid by the consumer, that depends on whether there is free trade in that article so as to bring it down to a living profit by competition. But in this case Mr. Bohn sells the papers as cheap as anybody else, but for the exclusive right to sell them pays so much to the United States, and a portion of the profits, which is regulated by his profits. This can be made very plain. Suppose the rate of interest was fixed at seven (7) per cent. by law, and a given bank should pay a large sum of money for the sole privilege of loaning money, which it might well afford to do, would a borrower therefore pay any more than seven per cent. on his loans because by doubling or trebling the business of the bank it made three times the profits, and could afford to pay one-third of the profits for the privilege, and still make a third more.

I shall deal with Mr. Bohn very strictly if I know of any attempt of his to enhance his prices beyond those charged elsewhere, because of the sum which he pays for his exclusive privilege of selling.

Your communication is respectfully returned, with reference to the indorsement of Captain Carroll, Provost-Marshal.

In reference to the matter of permission to bring books into this Department, that stands upon the same ground as all other merchandise. This being an insurrectionary district, by trade regulations nothing can be sent into it of any sort for sale without a permit from my headquarters, and this regulation exists all over the revolted States, and these permits are always granted upon application of reputable people.

By an examination of the Treasury Regulations at the Custom House, you will be able to ascertain the rules about this matter. At least, certain it is that I cannot spend more time in instructing you in the Trade Regulations of the Treasury Department.

I have the honor to be, sir,
Very respectfully,
Your obedient servant,
BENJAMIN F. BUTLER,
Major-General Commanding.

To Sinclair Tousey, Esq, President American News Co., 121 Nassau street, New York.

NEW YORK, April 26, 1864.
Major-General B. F. Butler:

Sir—Absence from the city has prevented an earlier acknowledgment of the receipt of your favor of the 17th.

We do not desire to trespass on your time and patience in discussing what you may consider trivial matters, but there are some points in yours of the above date, that seem to call for, or at least invite, a reply.

You admit that the tax on any article is paid by the consumer, and then go on to justify that admission by stating that "that depends on whether there is free trade in that article, so as to bring it down to a living profit by competition," which you attempt to show is the case in the matter under consideration, by stating that "Mr. Bohn sells the papers as cheap as any one else." That is just the point, General. We do not doubt that, but Mr. B. nor any one else can or will sell as cheap with a tax to pay as without one, and that is our cause of complaint. Let us illustrate. Before a tax was levied, and before this exclusive privilege was given, any dealer in your department could send to this city and Philadelphia and Baltimore, and buy the papers wanted, at as low a price as Mr. B. now buys them in those cities; but now, under your exclusive system, none of the dealers buy direct from the producers. Why? Because they cannot sell in your department, except by paying a profit to Mr. B., and that profit must come from the consumer, who buys from the middle-man, that your system obliges to buy from Bohn. We note what your Provost-Marshal says on this point, but it is not satisfactory. He says that "Mr. Bohn's agent informs him that no increase has been made in the price of papers." We respectfully suggest that an accused party is not always the proper witness as to his own guilt or innocence. If information was sought for beyond this source, as to former and present prices, by asking the newsboys, peddlers, and consumers, and others interested in the matter, more perfect information would be obtained, and here allow us to intimate, very respectfully, that we think you have not given this matter the attention it deserves, nor such as you usually pay to matters coming under your notice.

The subject is one of much importance to the Loyal Press of the country, as well as to the reading people in your department.

You further attempt to show that Mr. B.'s exclusive right causes no increase of prices, by supposing that the borrowers of money would not have to pay more than a fixed rate of interest in case the exclusive right to loan money was confined to one bank, which assumption is based on the fact that the rate of interest is fixed by law. Are we to understand by this that you have fixed the prices of papers, &c., in your department ? If you have not, the argument does not apply, and if you have thus established prices, then we ask that all persons may have the right to sell at those prices without paying tribute to Mr. Bohn.

But a word more on this exclusive right of the one bank to loan money. It is an old and true business adage that "competition benefits trade." Can there be any competition where there is no opposition ? If there are two lenders seeking investments for their capital, does not a borrower stand a better chance to get a cheap loan than if there were but one lender ? True, neither can get but the legal interest, but if there is more than one, one may take less than the regular rate rather than to have his capital remain idle. Apply this principle to the case under consideration and you have another reason for removing the restrictions now placed on the sales of papers in your department.

There are several points in our former letter that seemed to us to be worthy a notice by you, but which you have passed by ; but there is one point in your letter that we shall not fail to notice, and that is the last sentence, which we think is entirely unworthy of and unbecoming a Major-General of the army of the United States, inasmuch as it is uncalled for and entirely uncivil.

We have endeavored to address you in a civil manner, becoming your position and our own self-respect, and if our letters have failed in their respect, it was accidental not intentional.

We conclude by again asking that the exclusive system of selling papers, as adopted in your department, be abolished, and the right to sell them be free for all, subject to proper regulations as to the character of the publication sold.

Very respectfully, &c.,
SINCLAR TOUSEY,
PRESIDENT OF THE AMERICAN NEWS COMPANY.

The objectionable restrictions were removed.

MEETING IN THE NINTH WARD.

(*From the Tribune*, April 23, 1865.)

A meeting of the men and women of the Ninth Ward was held last evening at Bleecker Buildings, to mingle their grief with the all-pervading grief which fills the land, and express their abhorrence of the horrid deed which plunged a nation into mourning. A large number attended, particularly of the fairer sex. The room was decorated with the sad emblematic colors of affliction. At the back of the platform were portraits of the fallen martyr, with the ever memorable words full of devout reverence of his Springfield farewell address inscribed beneath. High above both were the defiant words of Andrew Johnson when in his place in the United States years ago he confronted the then dark conspirators, and in a short time afterward open traitors : " Show me a man who makes war on our Government and I will show you a traitor. If I were President of the United States, when tried and convicted, by the eternal God I would have him hung." Mr. John Wilson was appointed Chairman and Mr. Irving Adams, Secretary. The following resolutions were offered by S. Tousey and adopted :

Whereas, The men and women of the Ninth Ward of the city of New York, here assembled, with their minds deeply impressed by the awful crime that has plunged a people in woe, by the terrible murder of the head of the nation, by the attempted additional butchery of the Secretary of State, cannot refrain from mingling their tears with their countrymen ; cannot refrain from giving vent to the feelings of grief that have draped a nation in the habiliments of mourning, and thus to express, in this feeble manner, their profound sense of the dreadful crisis through which we are now passing ; therefore be it

Resolved, That, though grief has struck us down, we are not despondent ; that though we mourn, we will not refuse to be comforted; that the star of hope that always lights the horizon of a trusting people, we believe still shines for us.

Resolved, That we utterly and completely condemn and abhor the crime we now mourn ; that we invoke the restless spirit, Eternal Justice, to publicly bring the red-handed, fiendish-hearted assassins before the lawful tribunals of an outraged and indignant nation, there to meet the punishment due their unheard-of crimes.

Resolved, That in this last great horror we have a fitting climax to the continued horrors of the diabolical spirit of secession, slavery, and the utter disregard and abnegation of all humanities that have characterized the rebellion from the striking down of the nation's symbol from the walls of Sumter to the striking down of the nation's head in the discharge of his great duties.

Resolved, That the spirit manifested in the long catalogue of barbarous practices for the past four years by those aiming to destroy the nation, evokes and shall receive our most hearty and thorough condemnation : that we execrate and loathe it and its aiders, abettors, sympathizers, and apologists, and we hope and trust that it and they may speedily and forever pass away from among mankind.

Resolved, That the trial which this nation is now successfully passing through furnishes another and more convincing proof of the strength and durability of our form of government—another and more convincing evidence of the self-reliance that a great nation has in itself, and that in the case of us Americans, the voice of the people is but the voice of God.

Resolved, That we tender the sympathy of sorrowing hearts to the bereaved family of our late President, whose virtues endeared him to the millions of his countrymen, and which "plead like angels, trumpet-tongued, against the deep damnation of his taking off."

Resolved, That we sincerely trust that it may be in accordance with the will of our Great Ruler to restore the Secretary of State to the great sphere of his usefulness.

Resolved, That to the new President who has been so suddenly called to as great a trust as ever rested on human shoulders, we pledge our support in his efforts to crush rebellion, punish treason, and restore our country to the blessings of prosperous and permanent peace.

Eloquent and patriotic addresses were delivered by Major Haggerty, H. Everett Russell, the Rev. Mr. Blair and Dr. Dowling.

The Rev. Mr. Blair concluded his address as follows : Let us now with more determined zeal and united devotion raise up our glorious Stars and Stripes, the emblem of our Union, the emblem of our victory over the foreign foe "on many a well-fought field," the emblem of our triumphs over rebellion at home ; remembering the names of the great and good that have passed from among us—Washington who established this Union, Jackson who preserved this Union, and Lincoln who shed his blood to cement it. [Great applause.]

———

At the regular monthly meeting of the Union General Committee (city of New York), held in May, 1865, the following resolutions, offered by Mr. Tousey, at the suggestion of Mr. Postmaster James Kelly, were unanimously adopted:

" *Resolved,* That this Committee takes great pleasure in tendering to his

Excellency, Andrew Johnson, President of the United States, its earnest and undivided support in his efforts to crush the rebellion, re-establish the supremacy of the laws of the nation, prevent treason by punishing traitors, restore peace and commercial intercourse throughout the entire Union, to promote the general welfare, and secure the blessings of liberty.

"*Resolved*, That our faith in the President, as manifested by our suffrages in aiding to elect him Vice-President, has been wholly confirmed by the sentiments to which he has given utterance since he has been called to the Presidency, and we assure him that we will manifest our faith in him by our works in support of his administration."

At the above meeting but few prominent Federal officials were present, and those who were there acquired no personal capital from the above resolutions. The majority of that committee, at the time referred to. were " conservatives." Early in the next month, some of the " radical " members of the party called a public meeting in support of the administration of Andrew Johnson, recently become President by the murder of President Lincoln. The meeting was called for Wednesday, June 7, 1865, and Lieutenant-General Grant was to be present. The conservatives considered this move by the radicals as calculated to take the wind out of their political sails; they therefore hastily called a special meeting of the General Committee for the Tuesday evening preceding the meeting called by the radicals. At their special meeting, June 6, 1865, a series of resolutions, laudatory of President Johnson were introduced by Mr. Abram Wakeman (then Surveyor of the port of New York) and adopted, after which the following occurred as reported by the *Evening Post* of June 7, 1865:

" Sinclair Tousey offered the following additional resolution :

" *Resolved*, That without desiring to interfere with the policy of the Administration, we respectfully beg leave to suggest that good faith and justice to the black loyalists of the South, as well as security for the loyal whites of the Southern States require that the official influence of the national authorities shall be exercised in favor of allowing the privilege of voting to the loyal freedmen ; believing that the future welfare of our country can be better trusted to the franchise of loyal black men than to disloyal whites."

Mr. John Fitch supported Mr. Tousey's resolution with great earnest. ness, as the only sure means of organizing and sustaining loyal constitutional government, and prevent future secession movements.

Mr. Hugh Gardiner was in favor of negro suffrage, but did not wish anything to be done to embarrass the action of President Johnson.

Mr. Tousey deprecated the reference of his resolution to the Committee on Resolutions. It was equivalent to killing it without taking the responsibility of so doing. This committee ought to take a decided position, and it would greatly facilitate the determination of the matter in the only way in which it should be determined.

The ayes and noes were called, and the motion to commit adopted by a vote of forty-four to twenty-five.

On reading these proceedings of the general committee, in this day's paper, Daniel S. Dickinson, the U. S. District Attorney for the New York district, expressed surprise that such a resolution should, at such a time, have been referred to a committee; and asked "if they (the committee,) would ever learn anything." He was in favor of the adoption of the resolution.

The meeting under the auspices of the radicals, was held on Wednesday evening, June 7th, 1865, and was the largest ever held in the great hall of Cooper Union. In addition to pledging support to the administration of President Johnson, the following resolution on "Black Suffrage," reported by Mr. John H. White, was, with the others, received with applause, and unanimously adopted :

SUFFRAGE.

Resolved, That we hold this truth to be self-evident, that he with whom we can intrust the bullet to save the life of the nation, we can likewise intrust the ballot to preserve it ; and we invoke the co-operation of the Federal and State Governments, and the people throughout the Union, to use all lawful means to establish a system of suffrage which shall be equal and just to all—black as well as white."

These two sets of resolutions are inserted as part of the history of the times.

ON THE DEATH AND BURIAL OF PRESIDENT LINCOLN.

(*From the Tribune*, May 17, 1865.)

WAS IT EVER PARALLELED?

To the Editor of the New York Tribune :

SIR—The year we are now passing through, this EIGHTEEN HUNDRED AND SIXTY-FIVE, stands out in grand, bold relief from all its predecessors. a Star of the first magnitude in Time's constellation.

It saw the end of the imperious Slaveholder's Rebellion.

It saw the end of American Slavery.

Its earliest flowers covered the bier of a nation's mu⁚

The sun and showers of its young mouths freshe⁚.
over the martyr's grave.

Its Spring-time witnessed the grandest funeral page⁚
ored the dead or graced the living.

It saw a nation, thirty millions strong, drop scalding ⸳f sor⸳
on the tomb of their slain Chief.

It saw his murderer's dishonored corse sunk in an unknown place, ere
the victim reached his grave.

It saw a procession of grief-struck mourners two thousand miles in
length.

It saw the Great Dead carried to his home by a Nation, in whose funeral train cities were pall bearers, military chieftains were corpse-
watchers, high civic functionaries guardians of his Bier, great Imperial
States chief mourners, millions of uncovered heads bowed in tearful grief,
as the mightly cortège wound its solemn march under the sun-light of day
and the torch-light of night, from the scene of active duty, to the quiet
rest of an honest man's grave.

It saw millions of a down-trodden race lifted to the dignities and re-
sponsibilities of humanity.

It saw those millions bowed down, and their heads bent with grief as
sorrowing as children feel at a father's grave.

It saw villages clothed in mourning ; towns draped in Death's insig-
nia ; great Cities suspend their traffic ; the busy marts of commerce
hushed with awe, while the silence of living death covered an Empire.
Fit expressions of grief for a martyr.

It saw the dwellings of the rich covered with costly badges of woe ;
and the homes of the poor draped in the more simple and eloquent sym-
bols of a People's sorrow.

It heard holy ministers of Christ's Gospel speak words of peace for the
murdered Dead, and of comforting condolence for the living.

It heard the heart prayers of sincere millions for the rest of the de-
parted, and that his death might not leave the nation in the utter dark-
ness of desolation.

It heard a nation of mourners chant solemn dirges in accord with organ
peals and thunder of artillery, over the passing body of the nation's
martyr.

If respectful, manifest sorrow for the dead, be any proof of civilization,
then did Sixty-five witness a greater and more perfect civilization than any
other child of Father Time.

5

As the days of Sixty-five rolled into weeks, and the weeks wheeled into months, the meridian of the year saw the people of other lands meet in sorrow for the stricken nation; heard their grief utterance, saw their ANNOINTED RULERS bow their heads in the awe of sorrowing sympathy, and for once a child of Time saw

"A world in tears."

SIXTY-FIVE saw in the mourned one the incarnation of Freedom-Loving Liberty-Preaching people, the impersonation of the capabilities and possibilities of Institutions based on the voice of man echoing the voice of God, in the recognition of human rights and manly duties, the Emancipator of a Race, and the Guarantor of their Liberties.

It saw in the "deep damnation of his taking off" the possibilities and capabilities of the barbaric system which the GREAT MARTYR had, with a pen mightier than conqueror's sword, condemned to utter destruction.

It saw the world-old conflict between Liberty and Slavery end in favor of Liberty regulated by Law; of Justice founded on Humanity; of Civilization based on Right.

Was it ever paralleled ?

THE UNION LEAGUE CLUB ON SUFFRAGE AT THE SOUTH.

(*From the Evening Post*, June 15, 1865.)

At the last regular monthly meeting of the Union League Club, the following resolutions were offered by Mr. Sinclair Tousey, and adopted only one member voting in the negative :

Resolved, That the Union League Club of the city of New York invokes the influence of the National Government in the establishment of a system of suffrage in the rebellious States, which shall be equal and just to all, without distinction of color.

Resolved, That a copy of the above resolution, signed by the President and Secretary of the club, be transmitted to the President of the United States and to each member of the Cabinet.